CANAL ZONE DAUGHTER

An American Childhood in Panama

Judy Haisten

the Peppertree Press
Sarasota, Florida

ISBN: 978-1-61493-085-3

Library of Congress Number: 2011945968

Printed in the U.S.A.

Printed January 2012

This book is dedicated to

Canal Zone Sons and Daughters

We had an amazing time.

For my children -

Jennifer, Alan, Jalynn, Andrea, Steven

The Panama Canal

Acknowledgments

I'd like to thank my father and mother, Edwin and Jean Armbruster for the courage to embrace life without hesitation. I'm incredibly fortunate to have you as parents.

I am grateful to my sisters, Margie, Debi, and Connie. I wouldn't want to live this story with anyone else. You are the best.

Thank-you to Cassandra and Kay for your early support and believing in this story. Without you two, this story would have remained untold. Thanks to Charol for taking the story to a new level.

I owe a debt of gratitude to my children and grandchildren. You continue to bring so much joy and happiness to my life.

A very special thanks to my husband, Phil Haisten. I love your constant support and quiet strength.

Finally, I have deep gratitude to God. I am truly blessed.

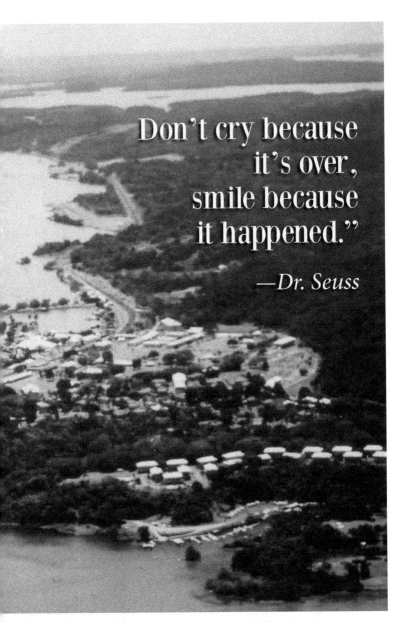

Don't cry because it's over, smile because it happened."

—*Dr. Seuss*

An aerial view of the small town of Gamboa.

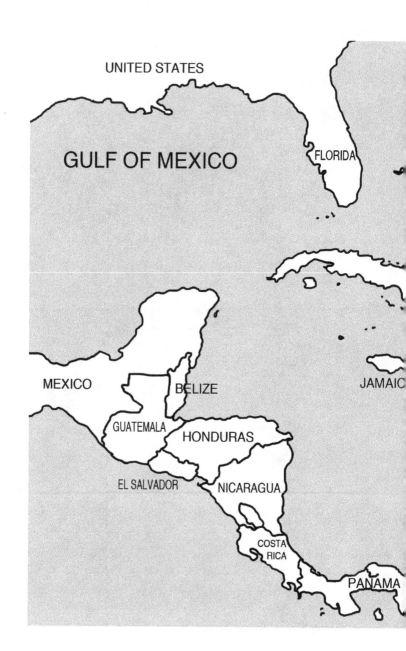

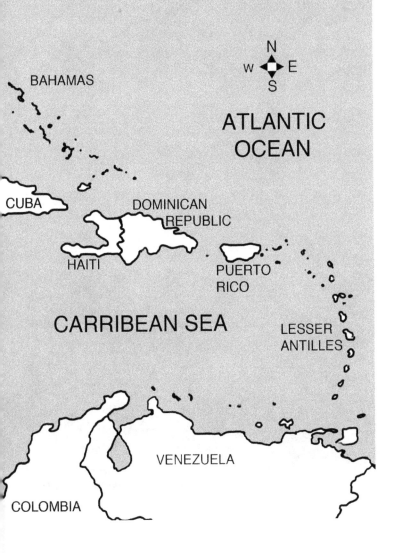
THE CARRIBEAN BASIN

ATLANTIC
OCEAN

BAHAMAS

CUBA

DOMINICAN
REPUBLIC

HAITI

PUERTO
RICO

CARRIBEAN SEA

LESSER
ANTILLES

VENEZUELA

COLOMBIA

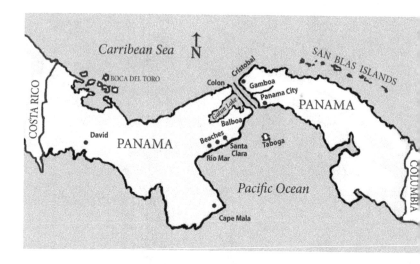

A ship passing by Gamboa; a view from the main road

Prologue

December 1989, six weeks after the fall of the Berlin Wall, I was in the kitchen cooking dinner and half-heartedly listening to television news. I was thirty, divorced two years, and had five children. A high-school teacher by day, I was pursuing a master's degree in education, so my nights were busy grading papers, studying, and refereeing my kids' arguments. While I cooked, the background noise of the news faded in and out of my scattered thoughts: what I needed to do tonight, when I would get to the library to do research for my final paper, and how I would get Christmas preparations done in time.

When the news anchor said, "Panama Canal," my heart skipped a beat. "Turn it up," I told my daughter nearest the TV.

U.S. Forces had invaded Panama. Dinner would wait. I turned off the stove and sat on the couch. My children stopped what they were doing and came to be with me as we watched the conflict play out. American GIs were swarming places I knew, walking streets I had walked, protecting people and land I loved.

Even after eleven years back in the States I wondered if I would ever be comfortable with my life here. I had often asked myself if it was because I had married so young or because my heart was still in Panama. The restlessness in my soul wouldn't be appeased.

I rarely talked about having lived in Panama. Many of my friends had no idea where it is, or that it's the narrowest point between the North and South American continents, or that this thirty miles of land separates the two largest oceans of the world. Nor did my friends know that thousands of Americans, me included, once called Panama home. Like my photo albums and scrapbooks, I had carefully sheltered away my memories of the Canal Zone.

Canal Zone friends now in the U.S. military were, with this conflict, fighting friends in the Panamanian Defense Force. My childhood classmates, John and Ricky, both in the U.S. Army and both had Panamanian wives with soldier brothers in the Panamanian Armed Forces. I wondered who had the right to decide that friends should fight against friends or brothers should fight brothers. Whose are the decisions that make friends and families enemies?

As film clips flashed across the screen of my small color TV, I saw familiar images of home. "Look," I said to my kids, "there's my old high school." Dutifully, they watched. "And that's where Grandma and Granddad live." Dad had accepted early retirement from the Panama Canal Company, but Mom was still a civilian employee of the U.S. Army.

"Will they be okay?" a worried youngster asked.

I reassured my children. "They'll be fine."

We had reports three days later on television news that all major fighting had ended, in an operation appropriately named "Just Cause." The U.S. forces shifted their role from fighters to peacekeepers, yet families once united were now split.

From Panama, my parents first telephoned my older sister, Margie, and then my younger sister, Debi, to let them know they were safe. Debi then called me, and I called the youngest of us, Connie. Our parents said they would tell us about the Panama conflict when they came to the States on Mom's leave next summer.

However, it was only a short time later that Mom's transfer to Ft. Bragg came through, so she and Dad sold their furnishings and bought a house in Fayetteville, North Carolina.

Maps change, and countries that once existed are no more. No longer would the Canal Zone be home for me, but only a place in my memory.

Gamboa
1964-1971

Our house in Gamboa

1

I was five in 1964 when we moved to the Canal Zone, a small strip of land under U.S. control in Panama—a Central American country more than 1,000 miles south of Florida across the Caribbean Sea.

Few people had ever heard of the 553-square-mile piece of America that was home to American citizens who lived on the five-mile-wide stretch of land embracing the Canal, a vital shipping waterway of global commerce. Here, American soldiers brought their foreign wives to live a life free from stares. Here, risk-takers dared to begin a life different from traditional hometown USA. Here, people who had made scandalous missteps came to start over. In the Canal Zone, all were on equal ground with no pasts and no prejudices.

My father had found a coveted job as an electronic technician for the Panama Canal Company. This subsidiary company of the United States government operated the Panama Canal, a 500-hundred-foot-wide ribbon of water that snakes its way through deep jungle connecting the vast Atlantic Ocean to the mighty Pacific deep.

I don't remember what we left behind—not that it mattered. We were far away from my grandma, cousins, aunts, and uncles. It was just Mom, Dad, Margie, Debi, and me. Connie wasn't yet born.

Our Panama house was made of thin wood, held together by 2x4s. Wide, open windows every few feet let sunlight stream onto the polished wooden floor and allowed tropical breezes in to cool the house. If I kept still, from beneath the overhanging eaves, I could hear air seeping through cracks in the walls, as if to escape the suffocating humidity and seek comfort in the shade of our roof.

On the glossy planks of that floor, I would dance in my stocking feet as gracefully as I could, imagining myself the best of ballerinas in a pleasing performance. My sister, Margie, would probably argue this point, but she never appreciated the fine arts as I did. After all, *she* was not taking ballet lessons in the kindergarten class in the back corner room of the Gamboa gymnasium and *I* was.

Gamboa is the name of the Canal Zone township, where we were assigned by the Panama Canal Company. Of all the places to live in the Canal Zone, Gamboa was the most isolated town on the Pacific Side. The only road into Gamboa crossed a single-lane, iron-and-wood bridge spanning the mouth of the Chagres River that flows into the Canal. Cars had to wait at a stoplight for their turn on the bridge, sharing the narrow space with a pedestrian lane on one side and railroad tracks on the other.

From the bridge, the road circled the neighborhoods and ended where it began, back at the bridge. Several side roads broke off from Gaillard Highway to cul-de-sacs and neighborhoods where pavement ended and jungle began. The train passed by the edge of town and picked up passengers at a rustic depot before continuing through the jungle bordering both banks of the Canal. Just past Gamboa, the large manmade Gatun Lake and unspoiled thick jungle split the Canal Zone into two provinces, ingeniously called the Pacific Side and the Atlantic Side

Newcomers might be assigned to live in Gamboa temporarily until a place became vacant in one of the more populated Canal Zone neighborhoods. The temporary residents often lived in small wooden four-plex apartments on the ridge overlooking the Chagres River. Dad's job was based in the Gamboa electronics shop, however, so we were assigned one of the town's permanent residences.

We lived in one side of a duplex on top of the hill across the street from the town's landmarked "red stairs," cement steps with brightly painted red iron banisters embedded in the hillside that provided a shortcut from our neighborhood to the center of town. So Dad had a five-minute walk to work and he often came home for lunch.

In 1964, the country of Panama was the home for Americans working in the Canal Zone and for twelve U.S. military bases, eight on the Pacific Side and four on the Atlantic Side. In some ways, the Americans in the military and those in the Canal Zone were integrated, but in many ways they were not.

The Canal Zone was a complete and separate entity. We had our own government, police force, postal system, and school system. We even had our own governor, appointed by the president of the United States. About three thousand American civilians made up a core of permanent Canal Zone residents. Canal Zone employees had independent and distinct roles specifically focused on operating and maintaining the Panama Canal. We called ourselves, "Zonians," and were not permitted the same privileges as military personnel.

Even so, we all enjoyed many physical activities. As a U.S. area, the Canal Zone boasted pristine golf courses, countless venues for boating and water sports, softball, baseball, shooting ranges, archery, horseback riding, and football. About the only things missing were snow skiing and ice skating.

Our American schools also had a fully organized curriculum of physical education. My kindergarten class included swimming and ballet during the school day, while high-school students took classes in bowling, volleyball, gymnastics, and table tennis. In addition, Canal

Zone students played basketball, softball, soccer, and tennis. Like other Zonians, I didn't simply learn about the sports—I played them, hard and seriously.

Gamboa's full-sized gymnasium was open almost daily from early in the morning until late afternoon. The large building was divided into sections. The front housed table tennis, free weights, parallel bars, and protective floor mats. On one side, a firmly anchored floor-to-ceiling ladder covered the entire wall. I spent hours climbing to the roof rafters, then racing back down the rungs of the ladder.

My kindergarten classroom was tucked in the farthest corner of the gym. A large fan stirred the warm, thick breezes that drifted through the windows carrying the unique Canal Zone scent blended of jasmine, wild orchids, mangos, bananas, ship fumes, mildew, cut grass, and who knew what else. If I could, I would label the smell and fit it neatly into some scientific category that could easily be understood by those of us who lived there. Like the Canal Zone itself, the smell was a contradiction: wild and tame, chaos and order, harsh and melodious, bitter and sweet.

The center of the gym was a full-sized basketball court with custom-built wooden bleachers on the back wall. The top bleacher framed the bottom ledge of the opened windows, allowing the welcoming breezes into the hot gymnasium. The constant whir of heavy industrial fans provided minimum relief, merely blowing the stale air around.

This was where the elementary students had PE exercises, tumbled, and played kickball and dodge ball. From the bleachers, proud parents watched countless square dances, flag routines, and ballet recitals. At Halloween, community members decorated the gym for costume parties, complete with a haunted house and witches' brew. During summer months, we Gamboa kids came to the gym when we had nothing else to do.

Mrs. Norris, our gym manager and PE teacher, was

there almost every day. Early in the morning during the school year, she would set up the badminton nets and Mom and a few other Gamboa ladies would play several sets before school started. By the time classes came for PE, the badminton nets were put away.

In the left back corner was the gym manager's office. Here Mrs. Norris had a large, standard-issue government desk with files, clipboards, and exercise charts all neatly stacked on the side. Several gray metal file cabinets stood against the wooden walls. Over time, the record of my own height, weight, number of sit-ups and cartwheels accomplished, and other important information were added dutifully to these files.

The other half of the gymnasium housed locker rooms and a manager's office for the Gamboa swimming pool, a major attraction. There were actually three separate pools, divided by cement paths. One pool was twelve feet deep with diving boards at three levels: low, high, and the tower. Parents and fans watched the frequent swim races from full-sized bleachers facing the pool. From inside the fence of industrial-wire that enclosed the entire pool complex, I'd wave to friends going to the clubhouse a few feet away or watch for my ride home, if I was lucky enough to get one.

It was at this pool that I tested for my B Badge—the absolute, most important test for any child living in the Canal Zone. It wasn't easy. To earn my B Badge, I had to prove myself by swimming the length of the middle pool, fifty meters. Then I had to tread water for three minutes, and float on my back and stomach before demonstrating other skills. The B Badge stood for Beginner Swimmer, but like the other kids, I wanted more. Later, I earned the Intermediate Badge and Superior Badge to prove my swimming prowess. Since so much of life in the Canal Zone was about water, swimming safety was paramount. The prevailing motto was, "make Zonian kids unsinkable."

The day I tested for my B Badge was my last day of kindergarten. I woke up before seven A.M. Hot sun rays already streamed through the screened-in window by my bed. I hurried into the bathroom while it was still unoccupied, yanked a school dress over my head, and slid on a pair of shorts under my dress. The dress was simple and plain compared to dresses I wore to church. School dresses had to be tough to withstand swing sets, monkey bars, seesaws, and dodge ball.

My older sister, Margie, was still in bed, with a light-colored sheet over her face to block the insistent sun. She was seven. Our bedroom had two single beds against opposite walls. Squeezed between the beds was a chest of drawers, three drawers for Margie, three for me. The vertical spacer separating the drawers marked our room's dividing line, not that one was necessary. You could tell Margie's side because her bed was made, her clothes were put away, and her books were lined up on her bookshelf. My side of the room was, well—different—and that's all I'm going to say about that.

Our younger sister, Debi, age three, had her own room. Our parents' room down the hall opened to a sunroom with a black-and-white TV, a recliner, and a daybed we used as a couch. The rest of the house was downstairs.

I grabbed a towel and a bathing suit from my laundry basket of clean clothes still waiting to be put away, tightly rolled the swim suit inside the towel, and secured both ends with large fat rubber bands.

Earning my B Badge was a proud day indeed. The laminated green card bore my name, Judy Armbruster. My first ID card, it symbolized independence. I now could go to the pool by myself. I was legitimately a Canal Zone daughter.

I celebrated the first day of summer vacation by walking *alone* to the pool. I handed the pool manager my B card and he pushed the button to let me in. Mom, Margie, and Debi joined me soon afterward to celebrate my new achievement.

That first summer in the Canal Zone, Mom, my sisters, and I spent most late mornings at the pool: playing Marco Polo, doing cannonballs off the low diving board, or reading comic books while lounging on the wooden-slatted pool chairs. I loved every minute of it.

CANAL ZONE SCHOOLS
SWIMMING POOL IDENTIFICATION CARD

Name.....Margie Armbruster.....
Age.....17..... ☐ Boy ☑ Girl
Town....Balboa. House.......... Phone.52-2503
27631 *Edith Haines*
Swimming Coach

A Panama Canal Swimming Identification Card (the B Card)

Armbruster family- Easter 1968- Gamboa Canal Zone

2

Two years later, when I was seven, my sister Connie was born. Dad had renewed his contract with the Panama Canal Company and our household, like most others, now included a live-in maid, Maria, and a tom-cat named Peanuts. Our lives had fallen into a predictable routine.

To make room for my new sister, Dad built a wall to divide the upstairs sunroom into a tiny TV room and a private bedroom for Margie, who was now nine. Her new room was barely wide enough for a single bed, a makeshift closet, and skinny chest of drawers, but she had her own door. Connie got the center bedroom, and Debi moved in with me.

Debi and I were almost alike, except that her thick curls were blond and mine were brown. We had the same brown eyes and dimples when we smiled. It was when I was seven and she was five that Debi and I became more than sisters. We became friends.

The TV room could only be reached through Mom and Dad's room—not that it mattered. SCN, the Canal Zone's only English channel, didn't begin broadcasting until four in the afternoon, mostly old programs donated by TV networks cleaning out their archives. However, occasionally the Armed Forces Southern Command Network would score a decent TV series or two, such as *Combat* and *Perry Mason*. When that happened, we'd all cram into the little room, elbowing each other for more space as we watched the grainy picture on our twelve-inch, black-and-white screen with its twisted rabbit-ear antennas. We didn't watch TV much, because there was more fun to be had outside.

We lived at the bottom of the hill on Williamson Place, where the road continued past a few more houses, before rounding a cement circle with manicured green grass and a humongous tree smack in the middle. In the late afternoons, my sisters and I joined friends playing freeze tag, ring-o-liveo, and kick the can at the circle. Lisa's house was on the circle and Bonnie and Kerry lived across the circle from her.

All houses were rented from the Panama Canal Company and, because there were no private fences to separate the yards, we never hesitated to cut through people's yards and driveways to save a few steps. The only boundaries on this dead-end street were natural ones and sometimes, we even ignored them. We roamed freely in drainage ditches, through the jungle, and on the banks of the Canal. We climbed up trees and ladders of lighthouses and jumped from bridges. Canal Zone sons and daughters were only limited by our energy and imagination.

In the opposite direction from my house, we struggled to ride our bikes up the steep hill of the road. Sometimes I had to walk my bike to the top, but the effort paid off when we raced on our bikes back down the hill! When we dared, we propped our feet on the handlebars and leaned back on our seats watching our wheel spokes spin beneath us. At other times, we'd go behind the houses and fly down the barren sides of yards, over various tiers of thick grass that made for a wild and bumpy ride! We had so much fun riding our bikes all day that we didn't stop until dark. In the Canal Zone, most families had an unwritten rule that we kids would be home when the streetlights came on promptly at six P.M. Not long after six, night settled in fast—not a lingering plenty-of-time-to-dawdle dusk.

By far the most fun we kids had was riding our bikes behind the DDT trucks as they sprayed the late afternoon air right before the streetlights came on. Every evening, when we heard the rumble of heavy trucks coming to dispense the mosquito-killing DDT, we rushed to our bikes. Kids who kept fish tanks outside would first stop to cover them with old towels so the DDT wouldn't get to the fish, then we were off. Oblivious to any harm, we pedaled as fast as we could behind the chemical-spraying truck, completely lost in a dense fog of insecticide. With ten or fifteen of us barely visible in the haze, our only concern was to avoid hitting each others' bikes. Debi and I would follow the DDT truck down the street, past our house, around the circle, and back, until with burning red eyes, we arrived at home.

On one such evening when Debi and I came into the kitchen after chasing the DDT truck, we found a small Amazon parrot standing on the long kitchen table, with Dad feeding him. The bird would take a little bit of food from Dad's fingers and turn in a complete circle before taking a bit more food.

"Meet Harry," Dad announced.

Harry walked across the table to us, as interested in us as we were in him. "Be careful," Dad warned. "He's still a baby."

"We have a bird? What about Peanuts?" I was worried about our gray tomcat, who was quite spoiled. Peanuts only liked being outside during the early morning and late evening, but during the day, he stretched across the entire length of the couch in front of the air conditioner and refused to move for anyone.

Dad mussed my hair. "We needed something male. Too much female power around here."

Debi and I giggled. Mom and Margie rolled their eyes.

"Well, Peanuts is male," Debi said. She put a little food on her own finger, and Harry pecked it off.

Dad laughed. "Not nearly enough to balance out this family." He held out a pencil for the small parrot to climb on, then put the bird in the large square birdcage that now sat on the floor in the kitchen corner.

We found it was silly to worry about keeping Harry safe from Peanuts. Harry bullied Peanuts. He chased Peanuts, pecked at him and flapped his wings furiously at him. Undaunted and driven by instinct, Peanuts would use his best stealth to sneak up on Harry, but there was no fooling that bird. He could sense Peanuts and would hold still until Peanuts was in striking distance. We watched Peanuts grin before Harry turned around. It was like a cartoon—Sylvester and Tweety. Peanuts didn't have a chance. In time, Peanuts and Harry came to a sort of truce, seeing that coexistence was unavoidable.

The outdoors offered all types of adventures. Debi and I both liked to ride palm-frond "horses." The tree halfway down the hill next to the red stairs shed the best palm fronds, just for picking up all over the ground. The dried fronds had a brown collar, a bent neck, and a long tail. We called the ones too decomposed "dead horses."

Sometimes we might see a great palm-frond horse that hadn't quite fallen out of the tree, caught on a branch. Debi and I would take a running start, jump high, and grab the tail end of the stem. The weight of our bodies would free the frond from the branches and holding our prized new horse, we would tumble down the hill. It might take a couple of tries, and we were usually banged up, but that never mattered to us.

Before we rode our make-believe horses, we had to look for thorns left on the stem. Once cleaned of thorns, a good palm-frond horse was hands down more fun than any store-bought broomstick with a fancy horsehead stuck on it.

One afternoon Debi and I had managed to free two new excellent horses when Dad was coming home from work and caught up with us at the red stairs. He walked over to the wooden bench at the edge of the hill that had a perfect view of the Canal, one of his favorite spots. Mom, Margie, and Connie joined us and we sat together on the bench. We watched tankers and cargo and passenger ships go by. The waves from a ship's wake slapped against the rocks as the sun slowly sank out of sight and as we squished each other on the bench. There was no place I would rather have been. Every few minutes a ship would sail so close that we could almost hear what the people on board were saying. At times, they waved to us and we waved back.

"Where do you think they're going?" Dad asked me.

I named every place I could think of: Mexico, United States, Japan.

Margie knew more places, but not because she was smarter. I knew it was only because she was older and had two more years of education. In time, I would be able to name all the places she could name and more.

3

Like many typical houses in the Canal Zone, ours was built atop concrete stilts, allowing air circulation underneath to keep it cooler. The space under the house included an enclosed single-car garage, a maid's room, a utility bathroom, and a patio. Some Zonians furnished their "underneath the house" like an outdoor family room, with rattan furniture and an old fridge. Other Zonians left their underneath-the-house bare except for the built-in over-sized cement sink and a washing machine.

After Dad hung a wooden swing from the floor joists under our house, my three sisters and I spent a lot of time sitting on it, talking, daydreaming, and reading comic books. During the dry season, it was a break from the op-pressive heat. During rainy season, we'd watch buckets of rain pour from the sky.

In front of both doors leading into the house were cement steps with a thick cement banister. Our front door, which only company used, opened into the living room. I always used the kitchen door. In the kitchen, Dad had built a counter and added top and bottom cupboards. He also built a bench along the length of the short wall behind our kitchen table. My assigned seating spot was on one end of the bench, Debi had the middle, and Margie the other end. Dad had a chair at the head of the table. Mom had a chair next to his on the outside of the table and Connie a high chair next to Mom, across from Debi.

A heavy wooden swinging door separated the kitchen

from the living room. In a back corner of the house, a staircase led to our three bedrooms and the one bathroom. I could race up those stairs two at a time, no problem, and with one bathroom in the house, sometimes that was a necessity.

We kept the house cool with ceiling fans and occasionally in some rooms, small window air conditioners propped up by sticks. The roof's wide extended eaves provided additional shade from the long reach of the sun.

Once in a while, when I'd ask Mom about her childhood home, she'd always say that she couldn't remember it. Dad told me that when Mom was young, she spent much of her childhood staying out of her alcoholic father's way and taking care of her invalid mother. Because her family was not considered respectable, my mother was all the more determined to be well thought of wherever she might be.

"You girls will not embarrass me," she'd say, pinching us hard when we misbehaved in public.

Mom told me that her mother had died when she was in high school, leaving Mom to figure out life on her own. With no one around to show her how to be the lady she aspired to be, magazines carrying the latest advice on how to be one of the beautiful people like Jackie O or Princess Grace filled our house. Mom wanted to know everything about such people and did her best to imitate their glamour and mystique. She kept herself thin and fit, too, and learned to apply her makeup with style. My mother instinctively knew that in a man's world, those who master the art of being a woman have the real power.

I watched, mesmerized, as she carefully set the short curly red wig on the Styrofoam manikin head—one of many wig heads cluttering the bedroom dressers, top shelf of the closet, metal file cabinet in the corner, windowsill, and even the far corner of the bathroom counter. More than once Mom asked Dad to build shelves in the bedroom for her wig collection, but he never did. I had no idea if Mom had more wigs than anyone else in the neighborhood, because that was not the kind of thing you asked your friends.

"So how many wigs does your mom have?" I imagined asking Lisa. However, I never asked, because she'd probably think I was weird. I loved visiting Lisa's house. Her father came from Iowa and was the fire chief in Gamboa. Her mother was Panamanian. Often Lisa's father wasn't home and then the air sparkled with rapid Spanish prattle. When I was there, her mother would speak to me in Spanish, slowly, and I would attempt politely to respond in a mixture of Spanish and English that made Lisa grimace. Her mother was patient, but also robust and matronly—nothing like my mom. I'm sure Lisa's mother did not have wigs.

I wondered if talking about wigs to other people was a sin. Many times when I asked Mom a question I considered a darn good one, she would sigh and then say, "Judy, you have got to learn not to ask private questions." I had a hard time figuring out what was a private question and what wasn't. It was just easier to keep questions to myself.

Mom loved her wigs and took great care with each one, because they cost money—something we didn't have a lot of. My mom was clever with money and she learned to be a sharp negotiator so she could have wigs. She didn't have as many dresses to wear to church as Lisa's mother and she often went without other things, but that was okay. She had wigs.

The day before the parent-teacher meeting night for my second-grade class, Mrs. Dufus asked us to describe our moms so she would recognize them. We were to stand before the class and, in two minutes, describe our mother. I panicked! What would I say? I didn't know what my mom would look like at parent-teacher night. Would she wear the long brunette hairpiece that she put the scarf in to blend with her own hair? Would she wear the short, blonde curls with long bangs that hung down on one side? Maybe she'd wear the jet-black silky wig she called, "the bob." If I described her as having shoulder-length red hair and she came to parent-teacher night wearing her platinum blonde Eva Gabor wig, would Mrs. Dufus think I had lied? I so wanted my teacher to like me, but how could she like someone who couldn't describe her own mother? I felt sure Lisa never had this problem.

I raised my hand, pointer finger sticking straight up to signal that I had to use the bathroom. Mrs. Dufus nodded. I let out a large sigh of relief and wondered how long I could be gone from the classroom.

I was in no hurry, but Gamboa Elementary wasn't a school where you could get lost—one hallway and one floor level, three classrooms on one side, two classrooms on the other with a small teachers' lounge, janitor's room, and two bathrooms for girls and boys at the far end.

Like Canal Zone houses, our old wooden school was built atop cement stilts. Underneath the building was an oversized cement patio with wooden benches, where we students could sit waiting for classes to start. In the floor joists high above, spiders created intricate webs and lizards ran freely. The year before, when I was in first grade, pounding hammers echoed in the upstairs hall as two new classrooms were being built underneath.

In the bathroom, I washed my hands for an eternity, then walked back to my classroom pretending to study the student artwork thumbtacked to the plywood walls along the way. I even sauntered into the janitor's room to delay my return, taking care the whole time to ward off bad luck by not stepping on a single crack in the wood floor.

Back in class, I was relieved to find the teacher had moved us on to math. It was my least favorite subject, but I concentrated on the blue-inked ditto worksheet on my desk as if it was the most interesting thing in the world.

There were seventeen kids in my second-grade class. In first grade, there were fourteen, but three kids had moved here during the summer. Except for the new kids, I'd been in class with the same people since kindergarten, and it would be that way until I left Gamboa Elementary in the sixth grade.

I had the best desk, next to a window. The school wasn't air-conditioned, but the wide open windows let the breezes flow through. Two heavy-duty room fans humming in the background circulated the hot air, a soothing sound.

Debi was luckier. She was in one of the new classrooms underneath the school, and they had air conditioning. It would be a few years before the rest of us enjoyed that luxury.

One of my big goals was to become a safety patroler. From my open classroom door I watched in the afternoon as four sixth-graders, in their patrol belts, left their classroom across the hall. I knew they would be lowering and folding the American and Panamanian flags that waved outside the school, the signal that school day was almost over.

Then five more patrol-belted sixth-graders went outside to position themselves along the cement stairway. We were not allowed to run up or down the stairs. If we did, a patrol guard would blow a whistle and call us by name. After which, we would have to *practice* walking up and down the stairs the correct way until everyone else except teachers had left for the day. I was called out for that enough times that it was no longer fun.

At last a sixth-grade patroler came into our classroom to press the button that rang the dismissing bell for school. One firm push of the button and the day was over! I dreamed about the day when I would be a sixth-grade patroler myself.

4

E ventually our parrot Harry learned to talk. Not only did he learn the words we taught him, he could imitate each of our voices amazingly well. His speech was as plain as a human being's, which often confused us. We suspected he deliberately played tricks on us. Sometimes Harry, sounding just like Mom, would yell our maid Maria's name. When Maria came running to see what was wanted, there would only be the bird. Harry wouldn't even hang his head in shame when she chided him in Spanish.

"¡Harry!" Maria would holler. "¡*Es malo!*"

He just squawked back at her.

Nor was Maria the only one Harry tricked. After he learned to mimic Connie's cry to perfection, sometimes he would cry like my baby sister when it was *my* turn to watch her. I would brace myself for the scolding that was sure to come and give him my meanest look. Sure enough, Mom would come running downstairs into the kitchen.

"Judy, why did you tease Connie?" She would ask, giving me 'The Look.' But then Mom would see that it wasn't Connie crying at all and she would laugh. "Oh, Harry, what are we going to do with you?"

No one was safe from Harry's mimicking. The parrot's games even drove Peanuts crazy. On lazy afternoons with Peanuts stretched out in his favorite spot on the couch, Harry would begin to meow just like our neighbor's cat. Peanuts would lift his head. Was another cat in his territory? It had to be. He would drag himself out of his siesta to investigate. If the kitchen door was closed, Peanuts paced back and forth in front of the door awaiting his chance. Then he would crouch low to the floor to peer through the narrow slit under it. Sometimes he nudged his head against it, trying to open it so he could chase away the other cat that was surely eating his food.

If the swinging door was already propped open, Peanuts searched every corner for the mystery cat that went on meowing until he realized the meow was coming from the bird cage. Then, on full alert, he parked himself next to the cage. While we all felt bad for our confused cat, Harry responded with fits of laughter. That's the sound I most remember from my home in Gamboa, Canal Zone—our parrot Harry's laugh.

Harry wasn't always confined to his cage. Only at night or when we weren't home did we latch the cage door. Other than that, his door was left open, and he was free to climb on top of the cage and stretch his wings. Sometimes when we were all at the table, he would flutter over and make himself the center of attention. We knew it was time to get his wings clipped when instead of fluttering he flew gracefully to the far end of the table. Just like a haircut, Mom got his wings clipped once a month or so, to keep our meals safe from flying feathers.

Then one day, the inevitable happened. Harry got out of the house. Debi and I were in the backyard playing marbles when we saw him flying around outside, having the time of his life. Startled, Debi jumped up and, to make sure it was our parrot, ran up the kitchen stairs and looked inside.

"That was Harry! He's not in here."

Mom had told us to be very careful about opening the door, since she hadn't time to get Harry's wings clipped. She even suggested we use the front door for a couple of days, but we were creatures of habit. Well, either somebody forgot or somebody didn't pay attention, because Harry was out.

He flew to a tall tree across the street and began singing high on a branch, taunting us from his new perch.

"Go get bird seed," I told Debi.

She ran back to the house and grabbed a handful. We walked over to the tree where Harry was perched. Debi opened her hand and cooed for him to come down to her.

He came down a couple of limbs, still too far up for anyone to grab him. He walked to the edge of the branch and peered down, looking at the birdseed. I felt a twinge of excitement and urged Debi to keep calling him.

She shushed me, "You're making me nervous."

I tried to keep still.

"Harry," Debi pleaded. "C'mon, Harry."

He straightened up, walked to the other end of the branch, turned, and walked back again, as if he were trying to make up his mind. Did he want the birdseed or not? He paced for a few minutes.

Then, with an unexpected rush, he flew down, grabbed some birdseed and was back up in the tree before Debi and I ever saw him coming. We had no idea a bird could move that fast. Still with a few seeds left in her hand, Debi called him again. Enjoying his treetop view, he ignored her. We needed help. Mom finally heard the commotion and came out to see what was going on. She saw us trying to persuade Harry to come down. She also saw that he was having no part of it.

"Who let him out?" Mom asked. "Not that it matters. You girls might not have a bird any more."

With her hands on her hips Mom surveyed the situation. "I don't know what your dad is going to say about this."

Another minute went by, with Harry watching us as intently as we were watching him.

"Do not let him out of your sight. I'm calling the fire department," Mom said, going back into the house.

Debi and I dared not take our eyes off our bird, which was not easy because his green feathers blended in with the leaves of the tree.

To our relief, one of Gamboa's fire engines showed up and two firemen climbed out and walked over to Mom and the crowd of neighborhood kids who were now gathering. Lisa joined Debi and me in watching Harry. It was a rare day for such excitement on our street. This was about as exciting as things ever got. This commotion would be talked about for days.

"Mrs. Armbruster," one of the firemen told Mom. "parrots live in trees. We don't get parrots out of trees."

"But he's a pet," Mom explained, "a member of our family."

Still that didn't cut any ice with him.

"If he were a cat," Mom pleaded, "wouldn't you rescue him?" She pretended to pick at a thread on her delicate white blouse.

Mom's logic had him stumped. Clearly a parrot, unlike a cat, didn't need rescuing from a tree, but Mom was so appealing the fireman wasn't sure what to say. How could he say no to a damsel in distress, especially one in a white short-sleeved blouse tucked into blue shorts, revealing smooth tanned legs?

Shaking their heads, the two firemen propped a ladder against the tree. Harry, spooked by the noise, flew to another tree. The firemen moved the ladder to that tree. One started climbing the ladder and had almost reached Harry when Harry jumped to the next limb just out of reach, cackling with laughter. Challenged, the fireman climbed off the ladder up a few branches into the tree, reaching for Harry. Harry waited until the man got close, then he flew to a higher limb out of reach. Several times, the game was repeated, until the frustrated fireman climbed back down and shook his head.

"There's no way we'll be able to get this parrot."

"You're just going to let our parrot stay out here?" Mom asked in disbelief, holding the hand of two-year old Connie, while her other three daughters strained their necks upward trying to see their beloved parrot.

Damsel in distress or not, the fireman started folding up his ladder. "It was a mistake to even try to rescue a bird in a tree. I don't know what else to do."

No sooner did he speak those words than Harry swooped down like an airplane buzzing a control tower, inches from the man's face, and back up to another tree.

The fireman grabbed his ladder and propped it up next to the tree Harry had chosen. "I'm going to get that bird."

Watching, Harry paced on the limb, then started singing and whistling a long, low wolf whistle. "Pretty girl. Pretty girl," he chanted.

The crowd of neighbors grew larger. No one wanted to miss this showdown between Harry and the fireman. Our neighbors knew what a prankster Harry could be, every one of them convinced that Harry knew exactly what he was doing. Our one concern was that Harry's natural instinct and innate sense of adventure would make him fly away.

The fireman did everything in his power not to let Harry's fan club down, unwilling to let a bird show him up. "You wait, folks. I'm determined to get this bird."

Harry kept watching as the fireman climbed closer. The crowd hushed. With his softest cooing voice, the gruff fireman pleaded for Harry to come to him. He showed Harry the birdseed Debi had given him. Harry eyed that birdseed. He eyed the fireman. He paced the limb of the tree. Then he flew on top of our neighbor's house.

Resigned, the fireman climbed back down the ladder. His partner suggested they go through the Copeland's house and up through the top window in the back bedroom. If one of them distracted Harry from the front, they might have a shot. The neighbors agreed this might work. We set out to trick Harry at his own game.

Our community hero raised the fire-truck ladder against the house. It wouldn't reach the top of the house, but we doubted Harry could figure that out. The fireman climbed the long ladder and called to Harry in a soft voice.

Harry peered over the edge of the house and watched the fireman. Meanwhile, his partner fireman went through the Copeland's house and upstairs to the second floor. He slid out the back window and crept over to Harry.

Those of us on the ground distracted Harry by making noises and calling his name. Loving the attention, Harry sang and laughed to his audience. Sure enough, the second fireman came up from behind Harry and grabbed his leg. Harry squawked and pecked, but the fireman held fast. He carried Harry into the house, unceremoniously plopped him into a paper bag, and folded it shut. Harry was caught. The crowd cheered when the battered fireman handed Mom the rustling paper bag.

Once safely back in his cage and locked in, Harry pouted. He turned his back to us. We tried to talk to him, but he put his head under his wing. He would have nothing more to do with us.

That night we all wrote thank-you notes to the firemen, which Mom delivered the next day along with brownies. And belatedly that day, Harry got his wings clipped.

5

On the road to the Ridge, tucked off to the side in the ever-present jungle, was Alligator Pond, a rather small pond surrounded by marsh with tall spindly grass guarding the edges. I was seven when I discovered Alligator Pond.

With another day stretching mindlessly before us, Lisa and I were rambling around looking for something to do. We walked past the lighthouse and down the path to the bridge, took a sharp left at the Quonset hut where the Gamboa Boy Scouts met, and headed up the paved road toward the ridge. We intended to visit school friends who lived up there, but the long uphill road stretched ahead of us, and we decided the ridge was too far that day. Instead, we turned to a barely hidden path to find that it led to a pond.

We sat on two rocks a few feet from the water. "This is where alligators breed," Lisa said reverently.

Like a true Zonian, I considered the water a new challenge.

I surveyed the lush trees and plants that framed the pond. Large spiders had created intricate webs linking branches and plant shoots. Tiny beads of moisture gleamed on the filmy spider threads, like warning lights. Mealy water bugs skimmed the surface of the stagnant pool. Foamy masses of frog eggs floated close to the bank. Natural instinct warned me that this placid pool of water could not be trusted. Nevertheless I asked, "How deep do you think it is?"

"You can't go swimming here," my friend said matter-of-factly.

Despite the shade of towering trees all around, the noonday sun bore down hard on our skin. Though the heat was oppressive, I really had no desire to get into the brackish water, yet something prompted me to boast, "I could swim it, no problem."

Lisa picked up a large stick and poked in the underbrush. "Some things are just stupid, Judy. There could be a crocodile right next to us, and we wouldn't even know it."

Showing my bravado, I got off my rock and walked to the edge of the pond. I put in a few toes, creating tiny ripples, as if trying to tempt a 'gator. The density and moisture of the vegetation created an almost mystical fog, and goose bumps rose all over my arms. My blood tickled. I took my foot out of the water. Lisa was right. Some things are just stupid.

"This is boring," I announced and headed back to the road.

Lisa scooted off her rock and followed.

Before long we were sitting in rattan chairs under her house, freeing our feet from sticker burrs that had easily found their way through our thin *huarache* sandals. With that done, I propped my barefoot-hardened feet over one chair arm and rested my head on the other arm.

Lisa sat the same way. "What do you wanna do now?" she asked.

"*No sabes,*" I said, hoping the Spanish ran smoothly off my tongue.

For the umpteenth time, my friend corrected me. "*Sé, chica.* The word is *sé.*"

I remained quiet.

The long walk in the hot humid sun had worn us out, and it wasn't long before we closed our eyes for a *siesta. Siesta,* now that was a word I knew without any correction.

6

Each of us sisters got sixty-five cents a week in allowance, if Dad remembered or if he had the change. The amount was determined by the cost of one movie, one item at the concession stand, and a tithe for church. Of course, we didn't have to go to the movies or buy a treat—we could save our money. Sometimes I did, so I could buy a comic book, but more often than not, I chose the movies.

Gamboa Movie Theater, a one-screen theater, showed three different movies every weekend, one on Friday night and two on Saturday nights. I usually went to the early show on Saturday, which started at 6:15. Most of the time the late movie was for adults and not very interesting or else, I wasn't allowed to go.

In less than three minutes, we could walk down the hill on the red stairs and be on the sidewalk that led to the movie theater. Debi and I would leave home as early as Mom would let us. If we hurried, we could meet our friends at the Gamboa Clubhouse before the movie started.

Like our school, our movie theater was a wooden building high on cement stilts. Underneath, thin plywood nailed to 2x4s enclosed the clubhouse, which served grilled food, popcorn, and candy. Here Gamboa kids would sit at the tables and tell jokes, laugh, and play table football with folded paper triangles, while we waited for Mrs. Suggs to open the upstairs door to the theater and begin taking our tickets.

After Debi and I hurried to find good seats, we made sure our feet didn't touch the floor, as we never knew what would be there or what might come our way after the lights went out. Propping up our legs almost at a jackknife angle, we found it quite comfortable.

I always sat as close to the middle as I could, declining the adventure of sitting by the open windows, for often the screens were torn and let in lizards or a wide variety of insects. A seat by the window also meant sitting next to the exposed wooden framing, where an unknown creepy-crawly or rodent might go scuttling by.

But seats in the middle had their own drawbacks. Many were broken, some obviously broken, so you just walked past those. You might not find out others were broken until you sat in them and bottomed out on the floor. Broken seats were common because of the "steelies"—steel ball-bearings that would come out of the seat mechanism if you knew how to get one. The steelie was a hot commodity. We played marbles every day at school and nothing, I mean *nothing*, beat having a steelie in a marble collection. Sometimes, if you had a steelie, you didn't even have to play. The person you challenged simply handed over the marbles. At other times, you had to take a chance. Even if you were only half good, with a steelie, you were sure to win.

Unless you were playing against a newbie, winning a steelie in a marble game was next to impossible. The best way to get a steelie was from a movie-theater seat. First you had to find an unbroken seat. Next, you had to bounce hard in the seat, over and over, just right until the seat broke and the ball-bearing fell out. Then you had to move fast to catch that tiny steel ball before it rolled down the theater floor.

With a wooden floor, everyone else in the theater also heard the steelie rolling and tried to grab it. No one would waste an opportunity to get a precious steelie. The little ball rolling down the floor was free game—until it was in someone's hands.

Of course, Mrs. Suggs heard all the commotion and came running, clapping her hands in rapid fire in an attempt to catch the person who broke the seat and get the audience settled down. Mrs. Suggs demanded order in her movie theater. Movies cost money, don't you know, and it was rude to be noisy and unruly. Getting caught breaking a seat or creating too much noise could mean instant expulsion from the theater. After that, I don't know what happened to a shamed movie-goer, because I never got that far. I was careful and I was fast.

Mrs. Suggs was so intent on catching kids breaking a seat or being rude that sometimes I was afraid to move. If she even thought you were doing something wrong, she would clap her hands like a machine gun, shine a flashlight in your face and say, "I'm watching you." She would also shine that flashlight in your face, if you talked or rested your feet on the back of the seat in front of you. It didn't matter if that seat was broken. No feet on the seats.

Even Dad had to obey Mrs. Suggs. Once he was with me at a movie and asked me to go buy popcorn. The film had already started. He must have spoken a little too loudly, because Mrs. Suggs clapped her hands, shone the light in his face, and gave him 'The Look.' He had to get the popcorn himself—I absolutely was not going to get on Mrs. Suggs' bad side. She didn't back down from anyone and she had the power to ruin your social life at the theater. No way would I mess with her.

Sitting in the middle section also brought movie goers another challenge. If you sat too far back, a bat might skim your head as it left the theater. The bats flew a straight course from the front of the theater to the back, escaping through open vents to the outdoors. Anyone sitting in the seats close to the upper vents risked a bat skimming her head. Not me!

It wasn't unusual to see bats swirling around in the sky outside at dusk or find them hanging from the eaves of wooden buildings. Gamboa is flanked by the Sobernia National Park and Barro Colorado Island, a biological reserve managed by the Smithsonian Institute. Close to one hundred different mammal species and one-tenth of the world's population of bats thrive in this area. Sometimes we even had to have bats removed from the inside walls of our houses.

The wooden posts mounted on the theater's faded wooden stage that supported the big pearl-hued movie screen seemed a favorite spot of the bats. On that same stage every year, my sisters and I performed Thanksgiving, Christmas, and Easter programs with our school classes. Once in a while, a magician put on his magic show there. At other times the stage was the venue for civic programs.

The bats would flap out of the large gap between the top of the movie screen and the bottom of the roof rafter when the movie projector light blasted onto the screen. If you sat in the first few rows you might not even see the bats unless you looked for them. A few rows further, you simply ducked as they flew by—the nearer the back you sat, the lower you had to duck.

At times a bat would get confused and fly around in the beam of light from the projector so that its shadow danced on the screen as the befuddled bat flapped wildly in search of the way out. We would holler, "Get out of the way! Come on! To the left! No! To the right!"

Mrs. Suggs would clap her hands and hiss, "Shush, Shush." The projectionist would shut off his machine, and we would groan and holler in the dark, even though turning off the light made it easy for the blinded bat to find its way to freedom.

I wasn't afraid of the bats. We accepted them as part of our movie-going experience, except for one particular time. Debi and I were watching the highly anticipated film, *Dracula*. In the first scene, a bat flies out of a tree and seemingly into the audience—filmmaking technique at its best. It so happened that at the exact moment when the Dracula bat came flying toward us, a *real* bat did the same. Debi and I crouched all the way to the floor. It took a long time to recover from that one.

7

The local buses opened up my world. The Canal Zone had two kinds. The Panama Canal Company owned the first kind, the old school bus type with drivers employed by the Company. Those buses served areas on the Pacific Side. I could get on one of them and go to Balboa, Gamboa, Los Rios, Diablo, or any of the military bases.

The second type was the Cheba buses, operated by the Panamanian government. These buses also had a few routes in the Canal Zone, but this bus system continued into Panama City and well into the interior of the country. Most of their passengers were Panamanians, who rode them to their Canal Zone jobs in the morning and home at night. Eventually, I rode both kinds of buses with complete freedom.

The first time I rode a Panama Canal bus alone was the summer between second and third grade. Mom had signed me up to take a "Reading for Fun" class at Balboa Elementary early in our summer vacation. The town of Balboa was a twenty-five-minute car ride from our Gamboa home and we were a one-car family.

Mom seemed nervous when she walked with me to the bus stop. It was my third time riding a bus, but my first time alone. On the walk, she repeatedly reminded me to take the big bus, not the colorful little Cheba bus. She explained that once I got close to the movie theater in Balboa, I was to say, "Bus stop," loud enough for the driver to hear. "Don't scream the words," she said. "Say them loud and firm." From the movie theater, I was to cross the street in the crosswalk and walk the few blocks to Balboa Elementary.

"I know how to get there," I reminded Mom. We had practiced that walk after church the Sunday before and it was straight down the street from the theater.

"After school," Mom continued, "follow the same road back to the bus stop outside the commissary."

I knew that, too. The commissary was exactly across the street from the theater. It was also where we did our grocery shopping.

"Look for the big bus, NOT the little bus," she repeated. "Make sure the word 'Gamboa' is spelled at the top of the bus. Do you know how to spell Gamboa?"

"Puh-leeze."

The big bus that had the printed wordstrip, "Balboa," stopped at the bus stop, and Mom talked to the driver. She gave me a few coins to put in the coin slot for the fare and a few coins to put in my pocket for the ride home. There were many empty seats on the bus, so I went directly to the back seat.

The last time I had ridden the bus had been with Mom and my sisters. Margie went directly to the bench seat at the back, because that was where the cool people sat. She always knew those things. "Quit following me," Margie had said sharply when I tried to sit by her. "Do you always have to do everything I do?" Miffed, I moved to the front and sat with Mom, Debi, and Connie by the window, so I could see outside.

This time the bus was almost empty and I could sit practically anywhere I wanted. I chose the last seat anyway. It was a bench seat that crossed the width of the bus. In the middle, you'd get the most bounce.

After Gamboa, the bus wandered around various housing areas to pick up passengers here and a few there. Most were Panamanian women with bulky cloth-wrapped bundles in their arms. I enjoyed hearing the happy, quick rhythm of the Spanish language and listened for words I knew.

"*Par-a-da*," one of the ladies said in a firm loud voice. I saw the eyes of the bus driver in the oversized mirror above his head. The woman who had spoken gave a little nod. We came to a stop, the woman got out, then we moved back to the road.

Before long, the same thing happened again. "*Par-a-da*," came a loud sound from a woman two seats away from the bus driver. Once again, the bus stopped, let out its passenger, and edged back on the road.

"*Par-a-da*."

For the third time, the bus driver stopped and let someone out. This time someone else boarded and took a seat.

I did not hear a single person say, "Bus stop." I tried to think. Did my mom say, "Bus stop," when we rode the bus together? I had to concentrate. We were almost to the movie theater. I was going to have to say something, but what? Immediately I started practicing in the back seat. *Parada. Bus stop. Parada. Bus stop. Bus stop* sounded stupid, but the word, *Parada,* wouldn't roll off my tongue. My mouth couldn't seem to form the word. I sweated and worried. Suddenly, without anybody even saying anything, the bus stopped. I looked around. We were in front of the movie theater. I looked up and saw the heavy brown eyes of the bus driver in the mirror looking right back at me.

"This your stop?"

I nodded, wondering if he had heard my thoughts. Then I remembered Mom talking to the bus driver when I got on. I was relieved. I would have time to practice my new word before going back home. I walked to the school, repeating the word *parada* to perfect my pronunciation.

The "Reading for Fun" class was over far too soon

and it seemed only a few minutes later that I was sitting at the bus stop by the commissary trying to determine which bus to take me home. This bus stop was different from the isolated bus stop in Gamboa. Many people waiting in a packed space under the overhang. Bulky buses rumbled noisily in a small turn-out at the side of the road with impatient drivers hurrying people aboard. Several Panamanians with shopping bags and packages scrambled onto each bus that stopped, while other buses tried to squeeze in to pick up their passengers.

I looked at the top of each bus for the sign that read "Gamboa," but I couldn't see anything. The buses were tall and the sign was at the tippy-top in black letters I couldn't make out. There were people going every which way, on the bus, off the bus, pushing, moving, crowding. Two Americans dressed in army field fatigues were lined up for a bus. I asked them if the bus was going to Gamboa. "No, Clayton," one said. The Fort Clayton army base was not close to where I needed to go. Another bus approached and I stretched my neck to see the letters on the sign at the top.

Someone in the crowd heard that I was asking about Gamboa and told me that it should be the following bus. So I climbed on the next bus, put my change in the canister, and hurried to the back. This bus had more people on it than the earlier bus, but I found a spot on the back seat with other cool people who liked to bounce.

Grinding its gears and rumbling, the bus pulled away from the commissary and edged into traffic. We passed nameless gray buildings and stopped at several small tin-roofed bus stops before we crossed the railroad tracks at Diablo and moved on past Albrook, Los Rios and Fort Clayton. The bus stopped and started, jerked and jolted, letting people off and letting people on. Americans and Panamanians shifted in their seats, shuffling and reshuffling packages and squeezing in when the bus got crowded, spreading out when passengers got off. I bounced happily in the backseat.

Soon, we passed Pedro Miguel and were on the two-lane Gaillard Highway paralleling the Canal. I watched Canal workers hook steel cables to a large cargo ship waiting in a closed chamber of the locks for the water to fill the chamber and raise the ship one level. Another ship had finished clearing the locks and was making its way through the channel.

By now I was the only American on the bus when the bus turned at Paraiso. We wound our way through the small township, one of the oldest settlements of the Canal Zone, and one time a U.S. military camp. Now it was the home of the black West Indian Panama Canal workers, descendants of the early West Indian workers who first built the Canal. Their community was separate from the communities of other Zonians, but the same neatly manicured lawns and standard cookie-cutter homes dotted the neighborhood.

At stop after stop, people got off, and nobody got on. Before long I was the only passenger. At the last bus stop in Paraiso, the driver turned, looked at me, and said with a heavy Jamaican accent, "Weeze you stop?"

"Gamboa."

"Tees booz no go to Gamboa."

"Where does it go?"

"Teez tee end a dee line. Weez go back to Balboa."

I wasn't sure what I was supposed to do next.

The bus driver told me I could wait for the Gamboa bus right there at the bus stop on the highway just outside of Paraiso. It would come shortly. When I told him that I had no more money to pay another fare, he nodded his head.

"I take you back to Balboa. You call your momma."

I moved to the front seat. The ride back to Balboa

was like the ride to Paraiso, only in reverse. The highway hugged the Canal, and I saw that the ship had cleared the lock chambers and was on its way. Another ship was ready to begin the process. We crossed the railroad tracks. We stopped and people got on, found their seats and settled in. I stared out the window and wondered how I was going to get some change and find the bus to Gamboa.

It seemed only a few minutes had passed when I was let off at the movie theater exactly where I had got off the bus earlier that morning. The driver told me to go into the clubhouse that shared the theater building. There I could ask to use a phone in one of the offices.

Putting my fingers in the large round dial holes on the phone, I dialed my home number 6843. Mom said it was a good thing that Dad was working at the Admin Building that day and she would call him. I waited by the phone for Mom to call me back. A few minutes later, she told me to start walking down the Prado to meet Dad. I hurried out of the clubhouse, walked past the post office and started down the street.

Meeting Dad renewed my confidence. "Coulda happened to anyone," he said. "Next time, ask the driver if he's going to Gamboa. Don't put your money in the slot until he says he is." I reassured Dad that he didn't need to come with me to the bus stop. Believe me, in the future, I planned to question each bus driver before I stepped on the bus.

"Is this bus going to Gamboa?"

"*Sí, señorita*. C'mon."

I hesitated a minute, not wanting to make another mistake. "I'm going to the red stairs right after the bridge. Do you know where that is?"

"*Sí, sí. Venga*."

I dropped my coins in the canister and watched them roll down in the slots. No one else boarded with me and there were only a few other people on the bus. This time I didn't sit on the back seat. Instead I went back a few rows and picked one of the three-seater benches and scooted over to the window. With the extra change Dad had given me, I had bought a candy bar from the vending machine outside the commissary. I opened the wrapper, broke the slender pieces of chocolate into tiny bits, and held each piece up in the light for inspection. I had learned the hard way never to bite into a chocolate bar, a cookie, or any other sweets without performing this ritual.

I'd learned that lesson on a day of running errands and grocery shopping with my family. My sisters and I each bought something from the commissary vending machine to hold us until dinner. My choice was a chocolate bar and I promptly ripped off the wrapper and bit into a creamy mixture of milk chocolate and peanuts. I'd eaten almost half when I spotted teeny white worms in the cream filling. Horrified, I showed Dad. He took my candy bar and studied it, turning it this way and that, then handed it back.

"They didn't eat much. They left you some."

I looked back at him unsure what to think. Margie rolled her eyes with an exasperated look, as if I had been put in her family for the sole purpose of disgusting her. And even though we were out in public on a cement sidewalk, Debi fell down laughing and squealing, "Eee- yew!"

Mom came to my rescue, "You don't have to eat that." She took the candy, threw it away, and handed me the last peanut-butter cracker from the packet she'd bought. I knew they were safe or Mom wouldn't have been eating them.

After that, I took all the care of a scientist in scrutinizing food from vending machines or concession stands. Nothing was more disappointing then spending your last money on something fun to eat and having to throw it away because some teeny insect had gotten there first. When I was confident that my chocolate was free of wormy bugs, I ate the pieces slowly, one at a time. Then I stretched my legs on the bus seat and propped my head on the window to let my heavy eyelids close.

"*Chica. Chica.*" The bus driver's voice sounded in my sleep and woke me. The bus had stopped, and there were the red steps on the hill that led to my house.

"*Gracias.*" Halfway home, I realized I'd never gotten to say my new word, *Parada*. Not even once. I guess it didn't matter. There would be another bus ride tomorrow.

8

Because Harry enjoyed the outdoors, when his wings were clipped and he couldn't fly, we'd take him on walks around the neighborhood. He perched on our shoulders and adored the attention, showing off by unfolding his wings to let everyone admire his beautiful colors. Our Amazon parrot flaunted and displayed his plumage without an ounce of shame.

Often we would set Harry's birdcage on the banister outside the kitchen door, where he would sing his heart out. Mrs. Dufus lived five houses down, and her parrot and Harry competed with each other to sing the loudest, until Mom brought Harry back inside, "Enough is enough."

One day Dad brought home quite a large walk-in cage to put under the house. The steel-mesh enclosure filled the space between the cement pilings that supported our house, fitting almost perfectly under the stairs. This would be Harry's new home. Dad said because Harry was no longer a baby, it was time for him to learn some parrot independence.

We wanted to give Harry a natural habitat like the zoo in Summit Gardens, so my sisters and I studied the encyclopedia in the hallway bookcase to learn what parrots liked, then did our best to imitate his native home.

We decorated it with all the trappings of the jungle, sure Harry's home would be the grandest home a parrot could want. We dug up tropical plants from around our

Judy sitting with Harry underneath the Gamboa house

backyard and planted them in pots inside his cage. In the wired-mesh, we wedged thick sticks for perches of different heights. Since the cage was tall enough for a child or two to fit inside, we put in a small bench where we could sit.

Having this new cage would give Harry the chance to be outside more and to spread his wings in a larger area. Most importantly, at least for us, we would be able eat a family meal without his constant babbling and interruptions. Pleased with our efforts, we felt absolutely certain that Harry would love his big new outdoor cage.

We were wrong! Harry hated his new home. Oh, it was fine when one of us girls was inside the cage with him, but the minute we left, he cried. First he cried like Connie.

When that didn't get our attention, he cried the way Debi used to. Then he would try another baby cry, one he must have picked up from the neighborhood. When he ran out of cries, he squawked as loud as he could—so loud we were afraid the neighbors would complain.

So we brought down Harry's old smaller cage and put it inside the big one. We thought that maybe if he went back inside his familiar home he would calm down. Each night, one of us girls would go down and put Harry on the little perch inside his smaller cage, shut the wire door, and cover the cage with his worn blanket. That helped some, but the moment the outside night noises started up, he would remember that he wasn't in the kitchen any more and start squawking.

"He's like a new puppy," Dad said. "We have to be patient. Eventually Harry will get used to being outside."

But Harry did *not* get used to it. In the morning after Dad left for work, Mom would sneak Harry back into the house. Back in the kitchen with the rest of us, Harry danced and sang, chattered and preened. Before Dad came home, we slipped Harry back into his outside cage, where he cried and squawked like a petulant child.

In time, Harry won. One evening as we were sitting down for dinner, with Harry going through his complete repertoire of crying voices, Mom, my sisters, and I all looked at Dad with the saddest eyes we could muster.

"What?" he said, exasperated.

"Nothing," we chorused. Dad heaved a big sigh, left the table, and came back with Harry in the little cage. He set the cage on its old stand, opened the wire door, and sat back down to his dinner.

Harry came out of the cage, stretched his clipped wings, glided over to the edge of the table and pranced around, sneaking a crumb or two that had accidentally-on-purpose dropped from someone's plate. Then he made a beeline for his favorite food—the butter. Mom managed to rescue that before Harry sunk his beak into the soft yellow stick.

Undaunted, Harry wasted no time in joining the family conversation with parrot chitter that no one understood. I don't know if beaks can really smirk, but I do know that Harry had a victorious glint in his eye.

Meanwhile, the empty cage downstairs begged for a new occupant. So when we were offered a kinkajou by friends being transferred to an Air Force base in the States, my parents said, "Why not?"

We got out our *Children's Book of Knowledge* encyclopedia to learn about this new little mammal and found out that kinkajous are sometimes called honey bears and live primarily in the rain forests native to Central and South America. We were surprised to learn they belong to the raccoon family and love fruit and honey, using their snake-like tongue to get honey from beehives and termites and ants from nested holes in trees.

The kinkajou's name was Honey. Before taking him home, we all visited him to make sure he was a good fit for us.

"Many people have kinkajous as pets," the owner told us, "because they're usually playful and docile animals." Right away, Mom was hooked. We all were. He hugged and snuggled like a cuddly bear, Mom said she didn't smell any wildlife odor and his soft wooly fur begged to be petted and stroked by little girls eager to adopt a new family member.

What didn't register then was that kinkajous sleep during the day and are most active between seven P.M. and midnight. Mom usually did all of her "town" errands late on Thursday afternoons, so by the time we had picked up Honey, talked with the owners, and loaded everything into the van, it was shortly after dark.

With us girls excited about our new pet, Mom began the

drive home. The two-lane road winding through the rain-forest back to Gamboa is dark and lonely. We never knew what triggered Honey into a panic. Maybe it was us girls whispering and giggling in the back seat, maybe it was the unknown car and new smells, or maybe it was the howler monkeys whose big voices all the jungle creatures could hear echo through the dense foliage. All I know is that our new kinkajou sprang onto Mom's neck, frantically looking for a way out of the van. Survival instinct prompted her to swipe at him with the back of her arm, and when she did, he clawed and bit down on it hard. More angry than afraid, Mom drove the van off the road, shoved us girls out, then got out herself. With her arm bleeding and four terrified daughters she flagged down a car, sent us off to get Dad, and stayed with the van and the roused kinkajou inside.

By the time the night was over, Mom had stitches to close the gash in her arm, and Honey had escaped. Remarkably, Mom felt badly for Honey. How would he survive in the wild? He'd been raised from a baby by dot-ing humans. Even more remarkable, Mom agreed to let Dad bring home a coatimundi to take Honey's place, just as long as *Dad* was the one to bring the animal home.

9

Coatimundis are also called coatis for short and, like
kinkajous, are in the raccoon family. However, unlike the kinkajou, coatis are alert during the day and like
to curl up and sleep at night. That was much better for our
family, since we also slept at night.

Once more, Margie, Debi, and I pulled out the
Children's Book of Knowledge and learned about this new
creature, which we called Cocoa. The steel-wired cage
was perfect for him to climb. We also anchored in several climbing branches, a thick rope, and a small potted
plant with plenty of foliage. Since coatis prefer to sleep in
a high place, we attached a platform near the top of the
cage. Then, we threw in a few cat toys. Coatis are curious
creatures and quite skillful at taking things apart. If we
didn't keep our coati busy, he would find his own way to
keep from being bored.

Like cats, coatis like to eliminate in one spot, so we
placed a small stack of papers in a corner to make it easy
for us to clean the cage. Of course, every once in a while,
we needed to hose down the cage and cement floor.

Cocoa's arrival turned our home life upside down. He
seemed to bring out new personalities in Peanuts and
Harry. The hard-fought truce between cat and bird was
now disrupted by this fun-loving animal that thrived on
mischief. After dinner, we would bring Cocoa inside for
an hour or two before we went to bed, but Cocoa was not
like a cat or a lapdog, content to snuggle close while you

stroked his fur, as Mom had hoped. Cocoa was more like a gremlin, far too active to sit on any lap. Instead, he frantically sniffed and pawed at anything and everything. His curiosity could not be satisfied. He loved to smell and he attacked any magazine that had a fragrant insert. We were amazed to see him turn the pages of magazines, then rip and mangle those that had a fragrance sample. Fortunately though, Cocoa, like a dog, understood the word, "No." When we firmly told him, "No," he generally backed off and found something else to feed his insatiable curiosity.

We had read that while coatis are very sociable and get along with other pets, we would have to be careful about bringing a coati close to birds, because by instinct, coatis eat birds. On Cocoa's first night with us, Harry took charge of putting Cocoa in his place and, just like Peanuts, Cocoa feared our parrot.

On the other hand, Peanuts and Cocoa played well together or at least we thought they did. A typical scene might find me practicing the piano, Harry turning circles dancing to the music, Mom and Dad on the rattan couch previewing Dad's recently developed Kodak slides, Connie rolling along the hardwood floor in her walker, Margie and Debi reading a comic book on the other couch, Peanuts cuddling on Mom's lap, and Cocoa sniffing and rooting in every nook and corner, his long tail twitching.

It never failed though that sometime during our peaceful family evening, the temptation of Cocoa's swinging tail would prove too much for Peanuts. The cat would pounce, and then the chase was on. They would chase each other in circles, until Cocoa leaped onto the curtains and flew from curtain to curtain around the living room, endlessly frustrating Peanuts. When either animal got close to Harry, Harry began to squawk and flap his wings wildly, and for the next few minutes magazines were knocked off tabletops and plants were turned over.

One of us would grab Harry, put him in his kitchen cage, and drape the night blanket over it to calm him down. Another of us would grab Peanuts and take him upstairs. With the atmosphere settling, one of us would sit on the floor with an open box or paper bag, and when Cocoa's natural curiosity drove him to poke his nose inside, we snapped his leash on and took him down to his cage so we could get ready for bed ourselves.

After school and on weekends, we girls took turns walking Cocoa. We never argued over who would walk him, because he never tired and each of us had the opportunity. Cocoa had been trained to walk on a leash like a dog, so we walked on the sidewalk while he sniffed and rooted alongside the entire way. If we ran, he ran, but in such a helter-skelter way that often our feet got tangled in the leash.

Cocoa loved people and our neighbors loved him. Sometimes if we forgot to latch his cage, Cocoa would get out, run to various neighbors' homes and scratch on their doors to beg for food or attention. They would tell him to go home, which he usually did. However, there were times when he wandered and we'd have to walk up and down the street calling for him until eventually he heard us and came.

One of our coati's favorite activities was climbing trees. Debi and I had a favorite tree in the side yard next to the jungle. Intending to build a tree house one day, we nailed a few boards onto several limbs. However, during certain times of the year, bulkhead black ants would swarm all over the tree. Cocoa took care of that—coatis eat ants. Debi and I would take Cocoa to our tree and let him climb and gorge on the ants. Then, with our way clear, she and I could safely climb up.

I think it amused Cocoa to have Debi and me in the tree with him. He climbed over several branches, ate his fill of the pesky ants, then came and sat on our laps. Debi,

Cocoa, and I spent hours together in that tree.

We also liked taking Cocoa sledding—tropical style, using a piece of cardboard as our sled. Sometimes a small crowd of neighborhood friends joined us for spontaneous cardboard "sled" races. By far, the best hill in Gamboa was on the ridge by the Golf and Country Club, but that was too far for us to walk. We had to be content with the hill across the street behind our neighbor's house.

When we had Cocoa with us, we took turns holding him on our lap and sliding down the hill. When we got to the bottom of the hill, Cocoa, ready to go again, would race us back up to the top. In the Canal Zone world, it was perfectly natural for two girls to hold onto a coatimundi and slide down a grassy hill on a piece of cardboard. Nobody thought anything of it.

One day toward the end of summer, Debi was pushing Connie in the stroller. I was walking Cocoa beside them.

"Do you have any money?" Debi asked me. I shook my head. "If we had money," she said, "we could walk to the

Cardboard sledding- a favorite activity with Zonian kids

commissary and get a comic book and some candy."

I got distracted by Cocoa rooting under some brush. My heart skipped a little beat when I saw that he had unearthed a coveted "hamburger bean," one of the jungle's gifts. The seed is brown, with a hard shell shaped like a hamburger and a darker brown fat line around it that looks like meat sticking out of a hamburger bun. When you rub the dark brown part on cement, that stripe becomes hot and can actually burn a red spot on your skin. Although I already had several hamburger beans in my jewelry box, I left Debi pushing Connie in the stroller and took Cocoa home right away clutching my prize.

I put Cocoa in his cage, ran upstairs, and started looking for my jewelry box that held my other beans. I couldn't find my jewelry box, but I did find the Barbie doll I'd been looking for.

"*Señora* Jean," I heard Maria call to Mom, "*la puerta.*"

Mom went downstairs to see who was at the door, and I heard Mrs. Tuttle's voice. Following Mom downstairs, I saw Mrs. Tuttle at the back door with Connie in the stroller. I heard Mrs. Tuttle tell Mom that Connie was her new baby, because she had bought Connie from Debi for two dollars. Mom and Mrs. Tuttle laughed. From the window, I saw Debi heading over to the red stairs. I slipped out the front door and ran to her.

"I got some money, Judy," Debi said. "Let's go."

"I heard you sold Connie!"

"That's right." Debi kept walking.

"You can't sell Connie."

"Why not? Mrs. Tuttle gave me money for her."

I couldn't think of an answer to that, so Debi and I went to buy new comic books and a candy bar to share. The rest of Debi's summer allowance went to pay Mom for buying back our baby sister.

10

When third grade started that fall, I struggled to make out the words on the chalkboard. I leaned as far forward in my seat as I could, but the white chalk letters still blurred. Mrs. Follett moved my desk to the front row, but that still didn't help.

"Judy," Mrs. Follet said, "if you can't see, walk up to the board until you can."

I spent a lot of time walking to the board, memorizing what was written, then hurrying back to my seat to write down the information. Mrs. Follet sent a note home to my parents and a few weeks later, I had my first appointment with an eye doctor.

Once Mom had the prescription in hand, our next stop was the dispensary, a small concrete building on the Prado by Stevens Circle, between the Balboa commissary and the post office. A room divider separated two waiting areas. On the left was the waiting room for immunizations where we got periodical shots for yellow fever, malaria, and who knows what else. On the other side was the waiting room to choose eyeglass frames.

When my name was called, Mom and I went into a closet-sized room with three of its four walls lined with rows of thick-rimmed, pointy cat-eye frames lining the walls. Choosing the right frame was of the utmost importance. Margie didn't wear glasses and she had made her opinion perfectly clear about being seen with a four-eyed sister.

Despite the number of frames, there was little choice in style. All were similar, although I could choose the color. At first the pink frames with the little jewel on the top outside corner caught my eye, but I finally settled on brown to match my hair. Maybe that way, my glasses wouldn't be noticeable.

With my selection made, Mom filled out the paperwork and paid the receptionist. It would take at least six weeks for the glasses to come from the States. In the meantime, I had to keep running up to the chalkboard to see the words and back to my desk to write them down as quickly as possible before I forgot what was on the board.

The day my glasses arrived was a bittersweet day. When I put them on, colors were vibrant and crisp. I hadn't realized how pretty nature really was. On the other hand, it felt like I was walking on the edge of a curb while peering through a windshield a few inches from my eyes. Any minute I expected to fall. I staggered and stumbled.

Mom encouraged me. "Glasses take time to get used to," she said. She wore glasses too, but only when she went to the movies.

No one else in my fourth-grade class wore glasses. I didn't want that distinction, so I did my best to avoid wearing them at all. I kept them in their case on the edge of my desk and when I needed to see the board, I'd take them out and, without unfolding them, peer through the lenses. After I saw what I needed, I'd put my glasses away and write everything down. I hoped no one noticed.

By the end of November, I wore my glasses full-time at home, realizing that my slightly altered appearance made no difference to the kids on my street, who weren't in my school class.

Lisa thought wearing glasses was fun and wished she had to wear them. She said I looked like a movie star with the pointed frames and thick rims. Margie's opinion was different. She said I looked stupid. "If you're going to wear those glasses," she said, "stay away from me and my friends."

When I complained, Mom said people had called her four-eyes, too.

"It's part of life, Judy. Learn to ignore mean words."

11

Paul said I could be on his team for the annual Christmas Tree Burn, but Margie wasn't pleased. She complained to Mom that third graders should not be getting Christmas trees for the bonfire tradition. That was for older kids.

"Don't worry about Judy," Mom told Margie. "If Paul said she can be on his team, she'll be okay."

Paul's family lived across the street from us. His father was a tugboat captain, whose family had befriended us the day we moved in. It was Paul's father who heard Mom's screams when she saw the oversized iguana on our banister. He couldn't stop laughing when Mom described the animal as a prehistoric dinosaur that had been hiding in the jungle all these years. Paul's family had been living in the Canal Zone for years and Mom's naïve but bold approach to living in a foreign country charmed them. Paul's mother, Darlene, told my mom details about shopping and living in Panama. His sister, Barbara, became our occasional family babysitter. So as far as Mom was concerned, if Paul didn't mind having me on his team, she didn't mind either.

"Just stay away from me," Margie warned. "I don't want you following me."

As this was my fourth Christmas Tree Burn, I knew what to expect. In Gamboa, as in all Canal Zone neighborhoods, the tree burn was the way we disposed of Christmas trees. Every year during the first week of January, each community held an organized bonfire in a large open field. The tree burn was the official end of Christmas break.

This tradition was one of the highlights of the year and now I would be a member of a team. That meant the end of being 'too little'—another benchmark of independence. Because Lisa was my best friend, Paul also accepted her on his team, reputedly the best team in Gamboa. We vowed not to let him down.

Paul took his role of leader seriously and held meetings in the underneath at his house to discuss tactics. First, we had to figure out where to store our trees. Paul asked if anyone had an empty garage or a maid's room we could use. We needed all the space we could get, because everyone would be scouting for trees.

We'd scout in various ways: knock on doors and ask neighbors for their trees, go out early on garbage pickup day to see if anyone had left a tree on the curb, or steal from rival gangs. However, for Paul, safety was paramount. No one on his team or any other team was to get hurt. Other than that, there were no rules.

We still had a few weeks before Christmas, so our first assignment was to knock on doors and persuade people to promise us their Christmas trees. Each year this was becoming harder, because many Zonians were turning to artificial trees. In the Canal Zone, we had to wait until the company ship brought Christmas trees and we never knew when they would arrive. Sometimes it would be two days before Christmas, so mobs of people would swarm the Christmas-tree lot.

Most trees that survived transport from the States were brown and dried out by the time they reached us, so we hid the deterioration by using lavish decorations on the brittle branches. The frustration of never knowing when the Christmas trees would arrive or the disappointment of watching a scraggly dying tree barely hold together until the day after Christmas had many Zonians buying artificial trees from the Sears catalog.

Lisa and I knocked on door after door, asking the occupants if we could have their trees after Christmas. We tried not to show our disappointment when our hoped-for contributors had begun using artificial trees or else had already promised their trees to someone else.

Lisa and I considered an artificial-tree owner a solid no, while a promised live-tree owner was a definite maybe. Maybe the kid who had been promised the tree wouldn't come back or maybe the Christmas-tree owner wouldn't remember which Gamboa kid had been promised and would think it was Lisa and me.

Lisa and I drew up a chart in our last year's school notebook. We noted the *maybe* trees in one column, with the few solid promises of trees in the *yes* column. Some neighbors had a policy of not promising trees to anyone. Instead, they set their trees out on the curb—up for grabs. Lisa and I made a third column in our notebook as well— these were on our *watch* list.

In addition to having to find trees, all team members were spies. This meant eavesdropping on opposing team members' conversations to find out where they planned to hide their trees. Everything was reported to Paul. By piecing together all our bits of information, we could find other teams' secret hiding places and hijack their trees for our own team.

Lisa and I buddied up with classmates who lived on different streets. Sometimes we pretended we were innocently visiting friends and would walk over to Jadwin or other neighborhoods. We were careful about what we said, because careless words could mean the loss of our own trees.

The Christmas Tree Burn wasn't our only friendly competition during the holiday season. Zonians also loved to decorate the outside of their homes. The first year my family was there, Dad scrounged up a few lights to put around our house. We'd been in Gamboa only a couple of months and weren't prepared for the intensity of the local competition. Some neighbors had grandiose scenery displays in their yards: large nativity scenes, hearth-fire scenes, Santa Claus, and sled scenes made out of plywood and colorfully painted for full glory.

Some neighborhoods, especially Balboa and Balboa Heights, worked together to create a Christmas wonderland that all Zonians enjoyed. Many times during the holiday season, my family would pile into our VW van and drive through the neighborhoods, listening to Christmas songs from SCN. As we passed the elaborately decorated tropical homes, we ooohed and aaahed and wished our house wasn't so plain.

One year, a few weeks before Christmas, Granddad came from Florida to visit. Because he was a sign painter by trade, Dad asked him to paint a winter scene like a Christmas card on a huge sheet of plywood. Granddad created a masterpiece. The billboard-size Christmas card hung from the landing at the top of our outside front steps and Dad placed a black-light in the bushes to illuminate it. The ultra-violet light shone on the bold fluorescent colors of the Christmas scene with the words, "Merry Christmas from the Armbrusters," across the bottom. My sisters and I were no longer embarrassed that our house was the least decorated on the street.

The day of the Christmas Tree Burn was as exciting as Christmas itself. Groups of kids brought their trees from various hiding places—garages, maids' rooms, secret clearings in the jungle brush. Borrowed trucks hauled some trees to the field between the school and the civic center, while several kids piled others on small red wagons and pulled them to the site. Still other kids towed the trees behind their bicycles. One year my friend, Keith, had four trees tied behind his bike, leaving a long trail of brown pine needles.

The team leaders counted their trees and proudly announced the number to all. The prize was the right to boast about the number of trees your team had collected and kept safely hidden. Stories were shared of how some boys had slept with their trees to protect them from other teams who didn't hesitate to use trickery to capture them. With all rivalries satisfied, friends were back to being friends.

In the late afternoon as the older boys piled some of the Christmas trees in a mound to begin the Burn, excitement built, and when night began to fall, one of the firemen lit the blaze at the base of the pyre. Impressive flames shot up high in the dark as the dried Christmas-tree branches caught fire. A glowing cloud from the embers enveloped us, and the air was heavy with the scent of pine.

Each time the intensity of the blaze lessened, more trees were piled on. Dragging more trees from their stashes, the older boys made sure everyone stood clear before they tossed them into the crackling fury of the flames. The re-energized blaze lit up the whole field and the elementary school. The hissing and popping went on for a long time as I stood by with the two trees I had managed to drag from our maid's room. Lisa stood beside me with her two, both of us at a safe distance from the fire until Paul came to take our trees and free us from the responsibility of guarding them.

After our trees joined the countless others in the blaze, Lisa and I drifted away to lose ourselves in the crowd. Pleased that I hadn't messed up, I felt sure I would be on Paul's team again next year. Only those who hadn't done their part would have to look for another group to join or else form their own team. As the immense blaze died down at last and the enchantment wore off, kids picked up the smaller trees and branches that had fallen by the wayside and threw them onto the fire. Younger kids circled and skipped around the dying flames.

Once the last tree was thrown onto the fire, the festive mood evaporated. An entire year would pass before we did this again. When the embers were ready, we roasted hot dogs and marshmallows, some of us even leaping over the blackened ashes where the flames had died. Adults gathered in small groups to talk about community events. Kids ran and chased each other around the field. Teams congratulated themselves for a job well done and began planning for next year's Christmas Tree Burn.

As the firemen walked around to make sure no missed embers were still smoldering, the dark of night quickly closed in. Not wanting the event to end, we Gamboa kids walked over to the movie theater and watched the late movie and for days after, the large burn ring in the field reminded us of our fun. But it wouldn't be long before the grass grew back to erase memories of past fun.

12

The first time I went to an overnight Girl Scout camp, I was eight. Debi was in the Brownies and too young to attend, but Margie was going. She made it clear that I was not to bother her and her friends nor put my tent anywhere near hers. She told me to stay with the girls my own age and do nothing to embarrass her. Margie, having been to an overnight camp before, knew the fun things to do, and babysitting her little sister wasn't one of them. Fine with me—I had no desire to be treated like a baby.

At the last minute, Lisa decided to go, too, having just joined the Girl Scouts in order to go camping. At our Scout meeting two weeks before camp, we had written a list of necessities to bring for the outing. Tents would be provided, but we were responsible for camp dishes, a cloth-mesh dunking bag for washing and storing our dishes, a bedroll made with sheets and blankets, a flashlight and a can of *Off* bug spray. DDT trucks didn't spray where we were going and there would be hordes of mosquitoes.

Scout Island, at the end of the Amador Causeway where the Bay of Panama joins the channel to form the Pacific entrance of the Canal, connects to the causeway by a narrow blacktop-and-gravel road over fill dirt from the Canal. Most days, a line of ships could be seen from the island waiting for a canal pilot to board and captain the ship through the waterway. At one time the island had housed World War II bunkers, but now part of the land was reserved for Scout campouts.

Masses of fully leaved trees with spreading interlocking branches crowded the place. Weeds, grasses, and ferns matted the floor of the jungle parts, punctuated by small grassy clearings dotted here and there in the otherwise impenetrable network. These clearings were the designated campsites.

Our troop leaders had reserved the largest clearing at the tip of Scout Island. A semicircle of tangled rainforest bordered the campsite. Thick grass blanketed the open ground, which ended abruptly at a rocky cliff above the junction of the Canal and the bay.

Lisa and I set up our tent to face the water, nine feet from the cliff's dropoff, to be shared with three girls from another troop. A shortage of tent pegs meant that each wooden spike had to anchor at least two tents.

Margie and her friends set up their tent further down the same waterfront row, and Margie, irritated that I had managed to secure prime real estate for myself, insisted that I move my tent to a back row away from the water. She informed me that places by the water were for more experienced campers. I told her I wasn't moving my tent, because there were no rules stating that first-time campers couldn't be by the water. Margie said all rules weren't written.

Shortly I saw her talking to the Scout leaders holding clipboards with pencils behind their ears. My name was called. I walked over.

My leader said, "Judy, Margie tells me you sleepwalk." Her clipboard held a drawing of the location of each tent with the names of girls penciled in by the appropriate ones.

Unsure what to say, I said nothing.

"Well," my leader continued, "did you walk in your sleep while your family was in Costa Rica? Is it true it took them an hour to find you?"

Except for the hour part, the story was true. That didn't mean Margie needed to tell people.

The previous summer, after visiting my grandmother in Florida, my family and I had driven back to the Canal Zone in our new van, a drive that took almost a week. It was the second time we'd done that drive and the roads hadn't improved. In Costa Rica, after we left San Jose, with no hotel where we could stop, Dad had to drive over treacherous mountainous roads for more than two hours in the dark. He hadn't wanted to do that part of the trip at night, because there were numerous, narrow one-way wooden bridges and pot-holed pavement with no guard rails or shoulders between the road and sheer drops down the mountainside, made even more crowded by people and oxen walking. It had been a tough few hours and when my parents finally found a hotel, Dad went in to ask about the price.

Long before that, I had climbed into the back seat and fallen asleep. Leaving me to sleep, Mom and my sisters got out to look at the ocean in the moonlight. Mom wasn't worried because she'd only be a few feet away. The way Dad tells the story, when he and Mom got back to the car, I was gone. They repeatedly called my name. Mom felt confident that I hadn't wandered by the water, because she'd just been there and if I had, she would've have seen me. Still, she retraced her steps by the water, while Dad searched the hotel grounds and surrounding buildings.

They both came back to the van and quizzed Margie and Debi. Had I been left at the top of the mountain when they'd stopped for gas? Who had seen me last? Did I get out for the bathroom at our last stop? Frustrated by their blank looks and no responses, Dad asked if they even knew they had another sister.

The thought of driving two more hours back up the treacherous mountain exhausted Dad, but Mom worried that if I'd been left behind, I could be alone in a strange country and in the dark for over four hours.

"Let's walk up the street a little bit," Dad suggested. "We have to make absolutely sure Judy's not here before we turn around."

Margie stayed in the van to take care of little Connie, while Debi, Dad, and Mom walked several blocks from the hotel calling my name, until they saw no point in going further. They concluded I must have been left at the gas station at the top of the mountain. Desperate, they were calling my name one last time when Dad spotted me down an alley, sitting on the lap of a Costa Rican grandma who was rocking me on her front porch. I was asleep.

"My sleepwalking was a one-time event," I told the leader. "It's not a habit." "I promise, Scout's honor, that I won't sleepwalk while we camp here."

With that, she relented. My tent did not have to be moved.

But Margie wasn't finished with me. "You know, Judy, there are sharks in the water," she said as we walked back to Waterfront Row.

"So?"

"So you if sleepwalk and fall in the water, you're done. Gone. It's over. I'm not coming for you."

"Okay."

"Just so you know."

By 6:30, darkness settled in and a campfire was roaring and snapping. Lisa and I followed other girls down the lane to the outhouse. Our small flashlight beams could hardly be seen in the dense blackness. Along the jungle-fringed road, the croak of deep-throated frogs chorused behind our nervous chatter. This would be our second trip to the outhouse and we wanted to get it over. I couldn't imagine using this latrine for the next two days. There had to be a better way.

The wooden outhouse was a short distance from the road and off in the tree line. In desperate need of a coat of paint, the building had two compartments, each with a door. One door had the word *Men* painted on it; the other door was plain. It didn't matter though. We could use either one, because both latrines were the same.

It had a tin roof, with a large gap between the roof and the boards that constituted the walls, and another gap at the bottom between the doors and the wooden floor. If the gap was to let out the awful smell, it also let in spiders, ants, and other small creatures.

I didn't want to be one of the first girls to go in. Let somebody else be the one to find a snake, tarantula, or raccoon. Nor did I want to be one of the last girls in, because by then the smell would be even worse, and I didn't know how long I could hold my breath.

Inside the shack was a raised board seat with two round holes, one hole for bigger butts, the other for smaller. Both were scary. If you were to fall through, no telling what would happen. Between the holes was a planked mini-screen for a bit of privacy, and another thick board separated the two compartments. Sometimes we'd call out to the person on the other side of the wall to make sure we weren't alone.

The wooden seat was shiny from use—luckily, no chance of getting a splinter when you sat. Your personal contribution dropped down the hole and we'd been told to use only a bit of toilet paper. Nothing to flush, no sink to wash your hands. Get in, get out. Fast.

By the time Lisa and I got there, a small line had formed. One girl at a time was entering each side. When each girl came out, we echoed relief that she'd survived. We also felt dread, with our turn getting closer. No one talked in that line. Talking might slow things down and we were in a hurry to get in and out.

Leaving the outhouse, Lisa and I vowed that so we'd never have to return, we wouldn't eat or drink until we got home. Of course that promise was broken the minute we found a couple of long sticks for marshmallows. With the other girls, we sat around the campfire holding our sticks in the fire and trying to avoid burning the bulging mass of white goo.

We ended the campfire sing-along with a mellow rendition of *Kum-ba-ya* and walked back to our tents, to find that our tent screening hadn't been tightly zipped, and there was an opening between the flaps. Now we'd have to check for scorpions and other bugs. One by one, we scoured our flashlights over the bedding and shook every piece out looking for unwelcome crawlers. Satisfied that everything was as we had left it—safe—we changed into t-shirts and shorts to sleep.

Then Margie appeared at our tent flap. "I wanted to make sure you all have your clothes on inside out."

Why had she asked that?

She kept on, "Have you heard of Tulivieja?"

Of course, I'd heard of Tulivieja, and Margie knew that. Often when we'd gone to the beaches of Rio Mar or Gorgona, we'd spoken of her.

"But Tulivieja doesn't come here," I said. "This is too far for her."

"Listen, she does come here," Margie said. "We're close to the water, and that's where she searches. Your only protection is to turn your PJs inside out when you sleep by water."

Surprisingly, one of my tentmates had never heard of Tulivieja. I thought everyone knew of the beautiful young Panamanian woman who had married a wealthy businessman. She had loved to dance and had gone to every party she could. After her baby was born, she couldn't go to parties like before. When her husband went away on a business trip and she heard of a party in a neighboring village, she dressed in her finest clothes and took her baby out to the woods by the river. Believing he'd be safe, she nestled the child in the roots of a tree, went to the party, and danced for hours.

Then a huge storm enveloped the village and rain streamed down the trees. The woman hurried back to her baby, but he was gone, swept away by the swollen river. The woman screamed and cried for her child.

I don't remember how, but the woman then changed into a hideous hag, with long wild hair and claw fingers—but every night she still searches for her child or any other child to replace her lost baby. She always looks for children who are sleeping by the water. If she finds you unprotected, she'll take you for her child.

Margie finished the story. I'd heard it countless times, but it still terrified me. After my sister left our tent, I turned my clothes inside out, for who needed to tempt fate? I could sleep with my clothes inside out the same as if they were right side. Without a word, Lisa and the others did the same.

13

For many people, a bird, a cat, and a coatimundi would be plenty of animals for one family, but Margie decided that we absolutely, positively, could not be a complete family without a horse. She repeatedly begged our parents, doing her best to persuade them. She spent many afternoons and Saturdays at the stables where she helped her friends take care of their horses and learned as much as she could about owning a horse.

"There's a horse for sale," Margie announced one afternoon. "It's only twenty-five dollars." Flushed with excitement, she'd just returned from the stables. Cindy was an older horse but still in fine shape—a perfect horse for a beginning rider. The owner's family was moving back to the States. Mom and Dad talked with other horse owners and learned the fairly reasonable cost of renting a stall and feeding the horse, so they agreed that, if Margie could come up with the money to buy the horse, she could have it. I suppose they thought Margie would never come up with that much money. She wasn't old enough to babysit, and there wasn't really any other way for a kid to earn money in the Canal Zone.

A few weeks later, Margie came into the kitchen with a check for twenty-five dollars. She'd written Grandma a letter and poured her heart out about how important a horse was for her, how she had been going to the stables and helping her friends take care of horses, explaining that a horse would help her learn responsibility, and that she could be a better sister by teaching us how to ride and care for a horse. Grandma was so impressed with the letter that she sent Margie a check.

I was so impressed that Margie had gotten money from Grandma that I wrote my own letter. I tried to remember all the words Margie had used and put them in my letter, too. I got a letter back from Grandma, but no check. She said that since Margie had offered to let me ride and care for her horse, I should be satisfied with that. We didn't need two horses. I supposed it was all for the best, since I actually didn't want a horse. I just wanted to be like Margie.

Margie took good care of her horse and went to the stables as often as she could to groom and ride Cindy. Sometimes I went to the stables, too, but to be honest, horses made me nervous. However, much as I tried to relax around a horse, I couldn't. Cindy was tolerant and patient, but my insides shook when I was alone with her.

Once in a while, Margie and I rode double, but not often. For one thing, she didn't like me hanging around with her and her friends. For another, my being uneasy on the horse made riding more difficult for Margie.

One thing I did like about being at the stables though. I could usually find a friend there to help pass the time. It was something different to do. Routines were tedious in Gamboa, so I welcomed diversions.

The stables were at the edge of the Gamboa Golf and Country Club built by Gamboa residents in the late 1930s. Riders trotted their horses between the bank of the Chagres River and the edge of the nine-hole golf course, tying them at times to a makeshift hitching post so they could come into the clubhouse for a soda and a bite to eat.

One day Margie and I tied Cindy there so we could go into the clubhouse. On one side was a nice restaurant that served full-course meals, while in the back was a large en-closed hall with a round King-Arthur–sized wooden table complete with wooden-slatted chairs.

One corner of that hall led to the kitchen, while the other corner led to a smoke-filled bar and grill. Kids weren't allowed in the bar, but we could either sit at the hall table or outside in chairs on the covered porch.

In the wall that partitioned the bar and grill from the rest of the room was a small courtesy window with a sliding door. Margie pushed the button next to the window, and the bartender opened the miniscule door, revealing part of his eyes and the bridge of his nose.

"Do you want something to drink?" Margie asked me.

"Yeah, but I don't have any money."

"That's okay. You don't need money. Watch this."

Margie ordered lemonade and a Coke. I watched her sign Dad's name on a slip of paper and slide it back to the bartender. In an instant, we had drinks and were sitting at the round table with friends from school, including Melissa.

Melissa lived on the Ridge and never came down to my street. It was too far. I liked sitting at the table talking with friends who lived near the Golf Club, so I stayed when Margie and her friends left with their horses. I told her I'd meet her later at the stables, and Melissa shared with me the wontons she'd ordered.

The next day I came with Margie to the stables, but walked the dirt path to the clubhouse. Melissa was already there. This time I got my own drink, a Shirley Temple, the same thing Melissa got, and signed Dad's name. We ate wontons, drank Shirley Temples, and chatted while we watched golfers putting and riders trotting their horses at the edge of the canal. After an hour or two, I walked back to the stables to meet Margie.

A few days later I returned to the clubhouse, but Melissa wasn't there. I wondered if I could order wontons with my drink and still sign Dad's name. I was a little nervous. Suppose I ordered the food, only to be told I could sign for drinks but not food? I sat at the table for a few minutes, working up the courage to put in my larger order and eventually went ahead to order wontons and a Shirley Temple. When the check came with the order, I signed "Ed Armbruster." The bartender accepted the check. It worked.

Later that week, at the clubhouse with more friends, I had trouble choosing between wontons or French fries. I decided to order both. My order came and I signed Dad's name. No problem. I generously shared my bounty with my friends. Margie came in with her friends and ordered a soda, but she left without even stopping at the table.

Several of my friends lived on the Ridge, so I only saw them during the school day. It made sense to invite them all to the clubhouse to hang out. I ordered hamburgers, wontons, French fries, and soda for everyone. We ate and laughed and enjoyed our feast. We promised to meet again in a few days.

We met again a few days after that and a few more after that. In fact, we met a lot of times that month. My group of friends grew larger each time. Being popular was fun!

Good things always seem to have to end. This was no exception. I was in my room, minding my own business, when Dad hollered up from the kitchen.

"Family meeting, now."

Debi and I hurried downstairs. We sat around the long kitchen table, elbowing each other and wondering what was up. Mom was standing at the counter. Dad sat at the head of the table. He narrowed his eyes at Margie and me.

"Girls," he said in a serious tone, "today, when I got my paycheck it was for only two dollars." He pulled out an envelope. "Imagine my surprise, when instead of getting money for my job, I got all these receipts."

He thought *he* was surprised. I was surprised, too. In

his hands were the slips of paper from the Gamboa Golf and Country Club, mostly signed by me, though Margie had signed some. It was a thick stack of receipts.

"Who signed my name?" Dad said, then waited.

Margie glared at me, then took the pile, sorted out a few slips, and handed me the rest. There was no denying my handwriting. For an uncomfortable minute, no one said a word.

Finally, I said the one thing I could think of, "They took this money from your paycheck?"

Margie acted all indignant, "What'd you think?"

When you're eight, you don't know these things. At least, I didn't. I blamed Margie for not telling me that the money would come out of Dad's paycheck or that there was a one-drink limit, only every few days.

"I don't know how you can be so dumb," Margie said, "or how we ended up in the same family." Glaring at me, she told Dad he could keep her allowance until her bill was paid. Easy for her to say, she had a small pile. No way was I going to offer my allowance. I kept quiet.

"Well, girls," Dad said, "will there be any more signed checks? Will I have a paycheck the next payday?"

I hadn't a clue. How could I? I hadn't even known these signed restaurant checks would show up in Dad's hand at our kitchen table.

With my line of credit gone, my glory days of sipping Shirley Temples and eating wontons with my friends from the Ridge were over. I didn't even go back to the stables for months or try to look up those other friends. Instead, I went back to playing with my friends on Williamson Place and reading comic books.

14

It was noon by the time my sisters and I managed to tear Mom and Dad away from their crowd of friends at church. Driving home during the hot dry season on Sunday afternoons was almost unbearable. The beating sun cooked us in our non-air-conditioned van. Usually, Margie and I claimed the window seats and opened every window, begging for a breeze to hit our faces. Debi and Connie settled for leftover oxygen. Sometimes Connie got so flushed that Mom let her squeeze into the front seat for fresh air.

Right before the bridge marking the entrance to Gamboa was a blind curve. All of us always sent up silent prayers for the stoplight at the bridge to be green. If it was red, Dad would possibly make a run for it. His rule was that if the other cars going in our direction hadn't reached the center of the bridge, he would go onto the bridge regardless of the stoplight's color. Then, with a little extra gas, he could catch up with the line of cars. If the cars were past the halfway mark he wouldn't take the chance.

That day we didn't see any cars ahead of us on the bridge, so Dad stopped, having no way of knowing how long the light had been red.

"Chinese fire drill!" Margie called with newly found energy.

Dad shook his head. "Ah, c'mon, girls. Not today."

Margie, Debi, and I climbed out. Connie stayed with Mom in the front seat.

"I'll leave you if the light turns green," Dad warned as we three ran circles around the van. We knew he would, too. He'd done it before and we'd had to walk across the bridge and up the hill. It was a long walk and much too hot that day to risk it. We ran faster.

Debi stopped at Mom's window and made a funny face at Connie. When she made it around to the driver's side and did a little jig, Dad impatiently waved her on. I came up behind her and grabbed her arm. "Let's get in the car. I don't think we'll make it one more time." I had no desire to walk the long way home.

But Debi took off for another round. It was just like Debi to push the limits. I stood at the passenger door. "Hurry, Debi, hurry!"

Margie already climbed back in. She wouldn't risk missing the ride.

Oncoming cars were getting ready to exit the bridge. Any second now, the light would turn green. Would Debi make her final lap before the light turned green? I don't know why she had to stop in front of the driver's side and do her jig again, but she did.

The cars coming off the bridge got closer and closer. If Debi didn't make it in time, I wouldn't get in either. I'd walk across the bridge, up the hill, past the lighthouse, and down our street with her. Not that Debi couldn't walk it by herself, but I'd go anyway. She'd do the same for me.

To my relief Debi made it back in time. We both collapsed in the back seat and shut the door just as the light turned green. Mom hid a smile as Dad shook his head. "You almost didn't make it," he said.

"We had plenty of time," Debi insisted, "even time to spare." She and I both secretly knew we'd barely made it.

At home, we each carried a paper bag full of groceries. Walking from the driveway to the back of the house and up the stairs to the kitchen felt longer with the extra weight. I was always careful to rattle and shake the thick brown paper before I held the bag close to my body, as a cockroach could be hitchhiking. Panamanian cockroaches were much larger than any cockroach I had ever seen in the States. It had taken just one such roach to crawl out onto my arm to teach me to be wary.

Debi carried in the fruit from the Chinese Gardens, one of our favorite places. The Canal Zone had several Chinese Garden stands. We usually stopped at Charlie's place down the road in Summit, on the way to Gamboa. Charlie's plot of land was right off the road. Any time during the day, we'd see at least one of his workers wearing a coolie hat and shouldering a long pole carrying large buckets filled with water. The Chinaman would walk up and down each row of lush green plants, dripping water through holes in the bottoms of the buckets. This sprinkling was done many times a day, even more in the dry season. Regardless of the time of year, the Chinese gardens were always vibrant and thriving.

Charlie and his workers spoke little English and less Spanish. "L-e-e-t-l-e Eeenglish," Charlie would say when we talked to him. He'd cock his head and listen intently to us. Even if he didn't speak English, he understood what we said and made sure that we had more fruit than we knew what to do with. In broken English, Charlie told us he was saving money to bring a wife over from South China, having come himself more than twenty years before.

For now, Charlie and his workers shared the upstairs of the wooden two-story fruit stand. In the front part under his house was a large table that held overflowing bins of fruits and vegetables. We loved to take deep inhalations of the sweet, fragrant, ripening fruit.

Along with the tomatoes, lettuce, and cucumbers fresh from the garden, Mom also bought oranges, tangerines, and pineapples that Charlie trucked in from Boquete in

North Panama. We picked bananas, limes, lemons, mangos, and other fruits from trees in our yard, but by far our favorites were Charlie's ginnups and Chinese plums.

The Canal Zone had many ginnup trees and we could have them for free. However, ginnups didn't fall from the trees like mangos and were harder to pick than limes and lemons, so we bought them from Charlie.

Ginnups were what we Zonians called them—later I learned they are also called mamones. The ginnup is a little ball of fruit covered by a thin brittle green skin that you bite into, but don't eat or you can use your fingernails to break through the skin. It's less messy just to bite.

Inside the shell is the seed. Roasted seeds can be eaten, but we were after the thin, yellowish translucent pulp. We'd pop a ginnup into our mouths and suck the gelatin-like strands of the sweet pulp. Ginnups are juicy and, when you bite into the outer shell, you have a battle to keep it from dripping all down your chin.

We'd always spit the seed out, and from a car window I could spit a seed almost to the tree line of the highway. We girls loved having a seed-spitting contest. Mom said it wasn't ladylike and we absolutely could not behave like that when Grandma or company was around.

When ginnups weren't in season, Mom often bought Debi and me a box of Chinese plums to share—twenty-five cents a box. Inside the colorful box with Chinese characters printed on the side were the dried-up brownish-red seeds covered with a thick leathery meat that sparkled with salt. Chinese plums had no outer shell like with the ginnups, but you couldn't bite into the meat, for it was too tough.

Sometimes the plum was so salty that we'd have to lick a tiny piece to desensitize our mouths. Often our eyes watered at the initial bitterness. Then we would suck on the seed to soften the leathery plum. Once past the powerful

Buying produce at Charlie's

puckering outer layer came the reward of an indescribable sweetness. Like the ginnup, when the seed had absolutely nothing left to give, we'd spit it out.

Nothing in the world compared to a good Chinese plum. For me, the enjoyment in the plum could last a lot longer than the enjoyment in chewing gum, though it was an acquired taste. After two or three seeds, my tongue would be raw from the harsh salt. Then I would have to wait a day or so before I could enjoy a few more.

A box of Chinese plums usually contained five little plastic bags, each with four or five plums. Occasionally, a box might have six little bags, which was like hitting the lottery. One time when there were only four bags in the box, I begged Dad to turn the car around, claiming we'd been gypped.

"Not so," said Dad. "All the times you girls have found six bags more than made up for any loss. Life works that way."

15

I was sitting on my bed reading comic books when I heard Debi running up the stairs. She barely glanced at me as she struggled to slide open one of her dresser drawers. Swollen and warped from the persistent humidity, the wooden drawer resisted her efforts. She banged at it with her fist, then gave it a strong kick. It finally gave in and she grabbed her bathing suit.

"Lisa and Kerry are going to the pool," she said. "You wanna go?"

I put down *Archie and Veronica* and got my own suit and we both rolled up towels.

Debi then searched the top of the dressers, under the beds, and on our desk. "Where's our B card?" With no card we wouldn't be allowed in the pool without an adult, no matter how many times we've been there before.

I went into our parents' room. Whenever Mom found our swimming-pool ID cards she'd put them on the corner of her dresser, but I didn't find them. I did find a quarter and a nickel, so I tore off a corner piece of paper and wrote, "*I owe you 30 cents. Judy.*" I put the note where the change had been. After we went swimming, we'd be able to get an ice cream at the clubhouse. Hopefully Dad would forget about my debt and not take thirty cents from my allowance next week. Sometimes he did forget. There were also time he forgot my allowance, even when I did my chores, so in my opinion we were even.

"Maybe we left them at the pool," Debi said. "Let's just

go." If the cards were at the pool office, we'd be okay.

We ran downstairs to the kitchen. Mom wasn't home, so we looked for Maria. She wasn't on the first floor, so we went down the outside stairs. There was Maria under the house, ironing clothes.

"*Voy a ...*" I started to say to Maria, then I stopped for a minute. "Debi, what's the word for swimming?"

"I dunno, I forget."

"*Voy a ...*" I repeated to Maria waiting for the word to remember itself. It didn't. I moved my arms to imitate swimming. Debi unrolled her towel and held up her bathing suit.

Maria watched us go through all of that before saying, "*Nadar.*"

"What? I mean *como*?"

"*Na-dar,*" Maria repeated, enunciating each syllable.

"Oh, yeah. *Voy a nadar.* I'm going swimming."

Debi and I started walking to the pool. We didn't notice the burning cement on our bare feet until we had crossed the street onto the cool grass. We then climbed over the protruding tree roots and stepped over the two single-file rows of cutter ants. One strand of ants was carrying leaves twice their size to their underground colony. The other strand of ants was marching out of the colony for another leaf from the tree they were stripping. Their work never ended.

Debi and I crossed the next street, passed the Union Church, and hurried through the field to the pool side of the gymnasium.

The office door was a Dutch door, top and bottom halves. When the pool was closed, the whole door was closed. When the pool was open, the top half of the door was open, allowing patrons to see into the office and out the back door to the glistening water. Smiley sat on the old chair by the metal desk against the wall. The Jamaican's broad smile revealed two gleaming gold-capped teeth.

"Whaz up, girls?"

I said, "Will you buzz us in?"

"Weetch one? The boys' locker room?" Smiley said with his usual grin. He got out of his chair, walked over to us, and propped his elbows on the thin shelf over the bottom half of the door. "You got youse cards?"

"No, we couldn't find them."

"Youse girls know the rules."

Debi gave Smiley her best smile. "Puh-leeze? Will you check in the box? I think we left them."

"Youse girls knows the office is no responsible for youse cards. Whaz you name? Square-headed rooster?"

"You know our names," Debi said.

Smiley leaned on the door, eye level to Debi. "I am an ol' mahn."

She looked squarely at him, unblinking. "Armbruster. Debi and Judy Armbruster."

Smiley's hand fumbled in the wooden box that held the cards. There was a slot for each letter and many of the slots had cards in them. He pulled out the cards for the letter A. "I have Margie's card, but not youse girls."

"Oh. She's at the stables," I said.

"Well, no cards for you. I can't buzz you in."

"Ah, c'mon," I pleaded. "You know we can swim. You know us."

"Rules are rules, girls. And this ol' mahn follows rules. I gotta keep my job."

Debi and I stood at the door with our rolled-up towels. Smiley went back to his desk. My sister and I stood there stolid, staring at Smiley, expecting. Finally he got back up.

"Okay, girls. Tell youse what I do. I buzz you in. Youse get you bathing suits on, then sit outside the locker room till a lifeguard can test you swimming."

The loud buzz sounded, the lock released and we

pushed open the heavy door. Debi and I congratulated ourselves once again for talking Smiley into letting us in without our cards.

We blinked, letting our eyes adjust to the dark room. The musty odor of mildew mingled with bleach saturated the air. Chipped green paint covered the wooden planks that separated small individual dressing rooms. Each contained a built-in bench and pegs on the wall. Debi and I found rooms next to each other and changed clothes, hanging our shorts and shirts on the hooks. Our bare feet soaked in the water on the wet cement floor.

It took only seconds to change our clothes and take a place outside the locker room. We waited and waited, but no lifeguard came to watch us swim. I walked over to the open back door of the office. Smiley was back at his desk.

"Smiley, when will the lifeguards test us?"

"I dunno, mahn. They got jobs to do." His eyes never moved from his paperwork. "They can't just stop to make sure you can swim 'cause you didn't bring youse card."

"You know we can swim," I reminded him.

"We got rules," he said, still staring at his stack of papers.

I kept on. "Did you tell the lifeguards we're here and waiting?"

"Yes'm. Just sit tight. They'll come when they get time."

Debi and I saw Lisa and Kerry swimming. We saw our other school friends splashing, racing, and doing handstands in the water. A couple of them got out of the pool and came up to us. We gloomily told them we couldn't find our cards. They nodded, understanding—many of them had been in the same situation. They jumped back into the water, "Come find us when you come in."

Finally a lifeguard motioned to Debi and me. We walked over to the pool, dove in, and swam the length of the Olympic-sized pool, while the lifeguard walked the edge of the pool beside us. After we reached the end of the pool, we had to swim back underwater. I swam the entire distance without coming up for air. Debi had to come up for air twice, but that was okay. After we finished our two laps, we then had to tread water for three minutes. Eventually, the lifeguard let us join our friends.

We played Marco Polo, dove from the diving boards, and played underwater tag. Then we heard thunder and looked up. The sky was darkening. *Please don't let there be lightning*, Debi and I silently begged, looking at each other.

But lightning did flash and sharp whistles blew everywhere. "Get out of the pool!" lifeguards hollered. "Get out, now!"

Some friends went under the overhang to wait out the rain, but this was going to be a heavy storm that could last an hour or two. Debi and I returned to the locker room, where we sat telling stories with Lisa and Kerry. When that got old, we changed back into our shorts and played hopscotch in front of the gym. Then we each pulled up a blade of grass and raced our green stems down the gutter. When the rain let up, we walked back home, our bare feet splashing through puddles on the cement sidewalk. My thirty cents jingled in my pocket for another day.

16

Gamboa had five churches for community members, but my family attended a church in Balboa across the street from the YMCA. There were times after church when we three girls would walk over and eat fried wontons while Mom and Dad visited with friends. Our congregation was a combination of Zonians and military families who preferred to attend church off-base. It was at church that I met Julia, whose father was stationed at Albrook Air Force Base.

She attended elementary school on the military base, but that made no difference to our friendship. We were both in fourth grade and both the middle kids in our families. We were the same height, had the same dirty-blonde hair and both were missing the same teeth. Even our names were similar. "We could have been twins," we said, proudly.

We attended church service in the morning and returned for another in the evening. Sometimes Julia came to my house or I went to hers on Sunday afternoons until the evening services.

I attended Julia's birthday party that year, and she attended mine. For Julia's birthday, we went to the SCN TV station and appeared on the afternoon kids' show, *The Skipper Andy Show*, the first show of the day. It started promptly at four P.M. Skipper Andy and his first mate, Happy Hoyer, welcomed us on their makeshift boat, "Lilac," and he interviewed each of us kids and asked which school we attended. That day I was the only kid from Gamboa. The others were military kids, like Julia. After Happy spoke to us, we stood at a pretend ship railing and waved to the TV camera. It was fun being on TV, even if I never did see myself.

For my birthday, Julia and I played musical chairs and tug-of-rope. We had streamers, balloons, and a Barbie Doll cake that Mom had learned to make in a cake-decorating class. That was the only cake she knew how to make, so we four girls always had a Barbie Doll cake on our birthday. We were able to choose the color of icing—so it wasn't quite the same every birthday, as Mom reminded us.

Julia's mom and my mom became good friends and shopped in Panama City together. While they were on one of their shopping trips, Julia came to my house to play. We had the whole afternoon, but soon we got bored and wandered down the street to see if anyone was at the circle. No one was. So we walked over to Clay Cliff, thinking we might find some people there. No one was there either.

"You wanna play on the cliff?" I asked Julia.

I'd played on the cliff many times. We neighborhood kids would play tag, run down the cliff, and skid to a stop right at the dropoff. Sometimes we would slide or roll down the cliff, getting clay stuck on our shorts and the backs of our legs. Clay Cliff had that name because there was no grass on it—just dirt and some rocks with trees on both sides. At the bottom were more trees and the single road in and out of Gamboa. A few feet past the road was the Canal.

Julia hesitated, "I'm not sure. This looks a little scary."

"It's not," I reassured her. "I've done it a hundred times," which I really had. Usually, though, there were other kids around. Today it was just we two.

"You go first," Julia said. "I'll watch,"

I went to the edge, walked down the familiar trail, and began to cross the cliff where there was only clay soil, no trees to hold onto. About halfway across the cliff, for the first time, I looked down. Until now, it had never occurred to me that I could easily fall and get hurt. I looked up and saw Julia at the top of the cliff. Debi had found us and was standing with Julia. After I looked down again, I began to feel nervous.

When I looked to where I'd just come from, I realized it was as far back to the tree line as it was to finish crossing to the other side of the cliff. I thought about climbing up to the top—but my feet wouldn't move. So many times I'd sat and joyfully slid down this cliff to the very edge. I felt silly to be so nervous now.

Julia hollered, "Judy, come back up!"

I wanted to, but my feet refused. I sat and cried.

"I'll rescue you!" she yelled.

She went to the fringe of the trees and made her way down. Then she, too, began to cross the dirt. Small pieces of clay pinged down the cliff, and Julia's foot slipped a little. She took care with each step and crept her way over to me.

I hoped when she reached me I'd regain my courage and we could get all the way across, but that didn't happen. Instead Julia looked down, then she looked up, then she sat down and started crying, too.

"Don't worry, Judy!" Debi hollered down. "I'll go get help."

Julia and I sat very still. We didn't want to move a muscle, in case it caused us to slide.

A few minutes later, Debi returned with Maria. I imagined Debi trying to explain to the maid what had happened. However, not knowing the words in Spanish, her only recourse had been to bring Maria.

"*Aquí.*" Debi pointed at me.

Maria gasped and talked rapidly in Spanish. Her hands flew everywhere. Then she started to cry, too.

That made Julia and me start crying again. If Maria was worried, maybe we were stuck here forever.

Maria yelled down to me some words in Spanish, then she was gone.

"What'd she say?" Julia asked me.

"She said to be still," I said. "She'll get us a rope."

In truth, I had no clue what Maria had said. I'd made it up because it sounded good and made us feel better. If we had a rope, we could climb back up the cliff. Actually, we could've climbed back up the cliff without a rope, because I'd done it many times before, but that was when other kids were here … and before I was afraid.

A few minutes later, we heard a fire-engine siren. *Just my luck*, I thought. There's a fire happening at the same time we're stuck. I couldn't believe it. We would have to miss seeing a fire because we were too afraid to move off this stupid cliff. The fire engine stopped below us, blocking cars wanting to come off the bridge.

Lisa's dad was driving the fire truck, so I waved to him. He waved back and hollered, "Stay right where you are." That was perfectly fine with Julia and me.

The firemen discussed the best angle to position their ladder. Then Lisa's dad looked up the cliff and said he'd climb up and get us without the ladder—which is exactly what he did.

In minutes, Julia and I were on the sidewalk at the bottom of the cliff. I told Lisa's dad and his partner we could walk home, but they said we could ride home in the fire truck. Julia and I weren't about to pass that up! We pretended we were in a parade and waved like carnival princesses as we passed people we knew.

Several months later, Mom said I could pick one dress from the JCPenney catalog for Easter. This was a real treat.

Julia convinced her mother to order the exact same dress. With great anticipation, I watched Mom complete the order form, then carried it to the post office. It would be seven weeks, but finally, Julia and I would be twins.

Julia's dress arrived the week before Easter Sunday. Mom said that Julia's dress arrived before mine because her dad was military and had a different mail system than the much slower Canal Zone postal system. Every day that week, I walked to the post office after school. Gamboa Post Office had only one clerk and he knew me by name. Every day I told him in my nicest voice that I was waiting for my dress from JCPenney to wear on Easter Sunday. Every day he said he understood, but there was no package for the Armbruster family.

On Easter, Julia wore her new dress, complete with white gloves and a white hat. I had to wear one of my old dresses. I had a white hat and gloves but, except for our family picture after church, I didn't wear them.

Two weeks later though, my Easter dress arrived. I called Julia, excitedly. That next Sunday, we both wore our dresses and we looked like sisters.

17

One afternoon Lisa and I ran home from school to change into shorts and t-shirts before running back to the gym. Mrs. Norris had the ropes down, so I wanted to spend every available minute practicing climbing. In a few more weeks, Mrs. Norris would have the work crew coil the ropes back up into the rafters until another season.

We'd been using the ropes for several weeks in PE class. I could climb a rope from the bottom knot to the very top and touch the rafters. Just as important, I'd learned how to slide down the rope properly so I wouldn't get rope burn. I could start at one end of the gym and swing Tarzan-style from rope to rope to the other end of the gym, but I couldn't quite make it back yet. Like the other kids in my class, I could climb halfway up the rope, twist the rope around one leg, and hang upside down, while a partner below me turned the rope in gentle circles. Holding onto two different ropes, I could easily perform front and back flips. Being on the rope was so much fun!

When Lisa and I arrived, a few kids were already on the ropes. We found two empty ropes side by side and sat on the knots trying to decide our first move. My neighbor, Paul, was playing basketball with his friends a few feet away. I waved at him and he waved back.

I got off the knot and holding my rope, ran sideways toward Lisa and jumped back on the knot, swinging high in the air. Lisa did the same thing, except in reverse swinging toward me. As we passed in the air, we grabbed arms and our ropes twisted around each other. Angling and contorting our bodies, we forced our ropes to unwind. Laughing, we did it again and again until we tired.

"Lisa," I said, "I'm ready to try the ultimate feat."

She knew what I meant. For the past few days I'd been watching the older kids climb the rope closest to the basketball hoop. In my mind, I'd rehearsed the steps several times. First, climb the rope to the same height as the wood-frame support over the basketball backboard. Then have a person on the ground pull your rope over so you can reach the beams of the frame support. Climb on the wooden frame, straddle the beam, and let go of the rope. On the beam, inch to the very end where it's connected to the backboard, then have your friend on the ground pull the rope back over to you. Standing on the beam, grab the rope and swing out. The kids I'd seen do this loved every minute of flying that far out holding onto the rope. There was nothing better, they said.

That day Lisa was hesitant, but I convinced her that I'd watched the other kids enough to know I could do it. So as soon as the rope closest to the basketball hoop was free I grabbed it and Lisa came over to hold the knot while I climbed to the support beams. Getting onto the beam was easy. I straddled it as I would a horse, then inched up toward the backboard. Everything went as planned until I looked down. I knew the rule about never looking down.

My legs felt weak and trembly. Halfway to the backboard, I took a breath and kept inching forward, but the further I went, the more my legs trembled. I knew I couldn't stand on the beam with trembling legs.

In all of my planning, I'd never planned on getting scared. Now I was unsure of what to do. *The next time I do a stunt*, I promised myself, *I will plan for what to do if I get scared.*

I needed to get down and rethink my plan, so I could ask the older kids what they did if they got scared. I also decided I'd wait until next year before trying again.

Inching my way backward was awkward, so I twisted my body as I tried to figure out how to turn around. That's when I slipped.

I don't remember falling. I only remember blackness and silence.

The silence broke when Mrs. Norris hollered about getting the doctor and calling my mom. That was the last thing I heard.

Somewhere in the void, I became aware of being carried. My eyes opened. I saw blood on Paul's shirt. I saw blood dripping onto the grass and through my inner fog, I heard Paul talking.

"I'm carrying you to the clinic. Five more minutes and we'll be across the field."

I closed my eyes and retreated into the quiet space. I liked that better than knowing my blood was going places it shouldn't. If I closed my eyes, maybe everything would go back the way it had been.

The next time I opened my eyes, I was lying on a white sheet in Gamboa's two-room clinic with the doctor aiming a large needle at my chin. "This will numb the area," he said, "so I can stitch your chin back together."

I closed my eyes, thinking I'd opened them way too soon. With luck, I would get back to the dreamy state before the needle got any closer. Minutes later, my chin was completely numb.

When I opened my eyes again, I expected to see Mom, but it was Dad who stood next to me, with a nurse asking him if he was okay. It seemed odd, her asking Dad that question, when I was the one lying on a stretcher with blood streaming down my chin.

Even though Dad was told to hold my hand while the

doctor put in the stitches, I didn't think I needed anyone to hold my hand, because I couldn't feel a thing.

The doctor must have read my thoughts. "I didn't tell him that for you," he said. "I need to make sure your dad stays with me."

I was amazed. How could Dad fearlessly walk through the jungle, shoot guns, and fly planes, but get white-faced and white-knuckled standing next to a needle that wasn't even going in his direction?

The nurse came back to tell us Mom had been paged at the Balboa Commissary and was on her way. Dad managed a nod.

When the doctor began to put the first stitch into my chin, Dad's grip on my hand grew tighter. I couldn't feel my chin, but I sure could feel my hand being squeezed. My hand was quickly becoming as numb as my chin. Mom needed to hurry.

That night Mom fixed spaghetti for dinner, but with my heavily bandaged chin, I wasn't able to chew. After the table was cleared Dad left the house and came back with a milkshake and two new comic books from the clubhouse. Tiny sips through a straw helped me to stave off hunger.

Mom said, "Looks like you'll only be eating oatmeal and mashed potatoes for a month."

"I'd prefer milkshakes," I answered through tight lips.

"I'm sure you would."

On Friday I stayed home from school and wished we had TV programs like at Grandma's house in the States. Since we didn't, I watched cartoons on the Spanish stations, read comic books, and did little else.

Then Margie came home from school and announced that the gym was closed. In deliberate tones, she told me there had to be an in-ves-ti-ga-tion. In the meantime, for PE, everyone would go outside for track and field. The gym wouldn't be open after school or on weekends for who knew how long, she said. She'd also heard that the ropes had already been put away and might even be taken down forever. She didn't say thank you very much, Judy, for ruining everything again, but that was the implication.

I flinched, knowing full well what she meant. A few days after Julia and I got stuck on Clay Cliff, a workman put up a fence around the cliff with "No Trespassing" signs. While technically we could still get around the fence, not many kids played there the way we had before and when we did, now we were trespassing. Was it possible that the gym would close forever, too?

On Saturday Debi and I played three long games of Monopoly. The heavy bandages on my chin affected my balance and Debi said they must have affected my mind as well—I was taking way too long to make my moves. Amazingly, Margie took a little pity on me, saying I was lucky that all I hurt was my chin and that when she got home from the stables, she'd play a game or two with me. So it looked like my immediate future would be comic books, board games, and Spanish TV.

That afternoon, Mom came into my bedroom. "I just got off the phone with Julia's mom, and you're not going to believe this."

Julia's family had been at the Albrook pool when Julia was horsing around with her little sister, Mary, and they both hit their chins on the cement edge. They both split open their chins and they had stitches—just like me. Now, there would be three of us at church tomorrow with bandaged chins.

On Sunday Julia, Mary, and I sat in a row in the same pew, all three with our chins in bulky white bandages. Julia and I even wore our twin dresses and it struck me that things aren't so bad if there's someone else who shares your problem.

18

Dad parked the car at the Jungle Survival School in Albrook Air Force Base where Julia's father worked, as Dad wanted to bring his Boy Scout troop there for a few hours of survival skills and to earn merit badges. He needed to make arrangements and sign official papers, and brought Debi and me along.

Jungle Survival School, one of several such schools in the Canal Zone, taught soldiers the skills needed to keep alive in places like Vietnam or South America. At this particular school, framed pictures on the wall featured Apollo astronauts with the proud instructors from the school who had prepared them to survive in dense rainforests if the need arose.

Thick tropical plants surrounded the school, some planted specifically to give students a first-hand experience. Anteaters, coatis, and monkeys scurried through the trees and bushes on the trails surrounding the concrete training building. Students at the school were taught that the spiny thorns of the black palm could stab and break off in the flesh causing a dangerous infection. Survivors could use leaves from the broom palm tree as useful shelters against a drenching rain or unforgiving sun. They had to know which vines could store up safe drinking water and which to avoid—not to mention the thin vine snakes that camouflage themselves in some trees, easily deceiving non-discerning eyes.

Trainees also learned what plants they could eat, such

as palm hearts and roots, and for protein, to eat bugs and crawlers from under rocks and rotting wood. They were taught how to build a lean-to and how to communicate in parts of the jungle too thick for radio communication.

When we left the car, Dad reminded Debi and me that we only had time to go inside the school, do what needed to be done, and leave. No exploring of the trails, and stay on our best behavior.

Our footsteps echoed through the tiled hallway that led to Julia's dad's back office. When Debi and I looked into one of the empty classrooms, Dad said we could sit at the desks there while he talked with Julia's father. We chose two desks in the second row, looking around at the pictures of plants and animals thumbtacked on the wall. Slips of paper under each picture identified them by species. The only furniture other than student desks were a desk and podium at the head of the room in front of the green chalkboard. The temptation of several long pieces of chalk in the tray was too great to resist.

I said, "Want to write our names on the chalkboard?"

Without answering, she silently nodded toward the door with her chin. I turned, stared, and saw a long, heavy-bodied snake slithering across the tile floor straight toward us. It kept coming closer and closer, blocking our only exit. As more and more of the snake came into the room, I'm sure my eyes grew larger and rounder. "Debi ..."

"It's a boa," she whispered. "See those markings on the back? They almost look like saddles on a horse."

This was no time for one of my sister's science lessons. With my heart in my mouth, I could barely breathe. We needed to get out!

Debi was still whispering, "Boas aren't poisonous, you know. They hide and wait for a rat or other animal to wander by, then they attack, grabbing the animal and wrapping themselves around it tighter and tighter until the victim stops breathing ... and dies."

Debi kept talking and the longer she talked, I felt sure her voice was attracting the snake. It certainly irritated me, plus I had an irresistible need to pee.

And still Debi kept on, "After the snake kills the animal, it swallows it whole. It doesn't use teeth to chew. The teeth are used only to grab and hold the animal, while squeezing the life out of it."

What seemed like a mile-long snake finally slid its whole body into the room, its fork-like tongue twitching from side to side, in and out of its mouth.

Debi finally stopped talking. She must have realized this was no pet from someone's garage. Wherever it came from, it was one enormous snake! Definitely not one to be satisfied with a mouse or two.

Soundlessly, the snake was still gliding across the pristine floor toward us. We did the only thing we could think of—quietly lifted our feet, propped them atop our desks and held our breath. I'm sure we had never sat so still in our lives.

Other people in the Canal Zone might have seen snakes wandering into buildings—I hadn't. Once I had seen a huge fer-de-lance snake stretched out on the banister of the red stairs in Gamboa, but that snake had seemed to be minding its own business, so I ran the other way. This boa was still coming closer, apparently interested in Debi's and my business.

Once before, Margie had seen a coral snake sunning itself on the steps outside our kitchen door. Walking down three steps before she saw the colorful snake, she hollered a warning to me to use the front steps instead and she went back into the kitchen.

Mom called Ground Maintenance to come get the snake, saying unless they did so immediately, she'd get the shotgun and take care of it herself. They came, all right, using a long pole to scoop up the snake and put it into a bag. Then the snake and the men left in a Panama Canal Company truck.

But this time, we couldn't call Ground Maintenance. Debi and I could hear Dad talking in the other room. I wanted to yell to him, but maybe if we kept quiet the snake wouldn't know we were here and move on. We sat there with our feet on top of our desks as the boa slipped in and around various desk legs, even prowling beneath us and on to the farthest corner.

Boas aren't fast. They're known to hide and ambush their prey, not to give chase. We counted on that fact. As soon as the snake was in the back corner, Debi and I jumped out of our seats to run, bursting breathlessly into the office where Dad was talking to Julia's father.

"Snake!" I squeaked out, my heart pounding.

Julia's father smiled, "That ol' snake is a mascot here. He wanders the building all the time. Won't hurt you a bit."

Debi had regained her bravado. "I told you," she said. "Can I hold him?"

Dad shook his head, "Nope. We're leaving now. Maybe another time."

In the car Dad said, "Listen to me, Debi. You can't pick up every animal you see. Don't forget, we live in a jungle. You girls must make sure you're jungle smart."

A few months later, Julia's father got transferred, so they would be moving. I hated to lose my friend, but she seemed philosophical about it. "You kind of get used to it," she told me when I went home with her after church. She sighed, "I'll be going to a new school again. Wish I could stay here."

What would it be like to have a new home every two or three years? I didn't want to find out, glad I lived where I did.

19

Whenever family or friends came from the States for a visit, Dad played the ultimate tour guide. Those were some of my favorite times, because I got to explore even more of the Canal Zone and the country of Panama. I noted everything I could.

Granddad always stayed a couple of weeks and Dad dedicated a corner under the house for Granddad's sign-painting supplies: a workbench with paints, paintbrushes, rags, and pencils, plus a couple of easels and a drop cloth on the cement floor. Granddad painted signs for the Gamboa Golf and Country Club, earning us the reward of a nice family dinner. He also painted signs for churches and local organizations, and sometimes they paid him.

When Grand-dad was visiting, I'd come home from school to find him sitting under the house, painting away and enjoying the fresh air. Painting outside suited him best, but he didn't like kids or animals. While he tolerated me, my sisters and Peanuts, Harry and Cocoa terrified him.

Worse luck, our coatimundi was fascinated by the paints and paintbrushes and seized every opportunity to jump on the worktable. He'd knock over jars of paint, dip his tail and paws in the liquid, leave his own smears of paint everywhere. Cocoa was tame, but he wasn't domesticated. Simply stomping a foot and saying, "Shoo!" didn't deter Cocoa one bit, so when Granddad visited, we had to keep Cocoa on a leash or in his cage.

One Saturday, Granddad wanted to ride the train to the Atlantic Side of the Canal Zone, enjoying the ride along the Canal and traveling through parts of the rain forest. The understanding was that we would pick him up at the train station in Colon. The Canal Zone roads were well-maintained, but the other roads that cut through portions of Panama were not well looked after, full of pot holes, so the drive took more than an hour.

While the Atlantic Side with its six small Zonian towns was relatively isolated from the rest of the Canal Zone, the same scrupulous care was given to landscaping, maintenance, and facilities, such as the public pools.

Like the Pacific Side, there were several elementary schools and one high school, but just four military bases compared to eight on the Pacific Side. During World War II there had been more military outposts, which they now stood empty.

Fort Sherman was home to the Jungle Operations Training Center. Over half of this small base at the northernmost point of the Canal was covered by the jungle. Dad headed there first, making the large zoo on the base our first stop.

To reach Fort Sherman, we had to cross the Canal at the only crossing place for cars, the Gatun Locks. The bridge there was actually one of the swinging gates of the third chamber of the three-chamber locks.

I never tired of this highlight to the trip. There was nothing like being one with the Canal locks themselves. While crossing the bridge, we could see into the locks and if we were lucky, a ship would be waiting its turn to enter into the lock chamber. Sometimes when we made this trip, Dad deliberately waited to cross the bridge until a ship was coming through.

On the other side of the bridge, the road paralleled the French Canal. Dad pointed this out to Granddad, telling him it was the French who had first tried to build a canal here. They had failed, but the Americans had succeeded.

The MP at the gate of Fort Sherman waved us through. Margie, Debi, and I debated which animal we wanted to see first at the zoo. Margie liked the black panther and spotted jaguar. Debi liked the monkeys. I found the sloths the most interesting.

In addition to its collection of exotic jungle animals, this zoo had one of the largest collection of snakes, including a huge anaconda, which pleased Debi immensely.

Granddad holding the snake at Fort Sherman Jungle Operations Zoo

She had begged and begged our parents for a pet snake, but Mom had drawn the line at that. Mom was game for almost all of Dad's and our antics, but no snakes. She didn't care how many of our friends' moms let them have snakes—she wasn't one of them, she said. Debi had to be content either to be with snakes at her friends' houses or visit snakes at the zoo. So there we were.

Debi insisted that we all go from cage to cage, admiring the different snakes as she talked endlessly about each one. At the demonstration area, one of the soldiers took out a large boa constrictor and allowed us to touch it, even to hold it. If we wanted, he said, he would put the snake on our shoulders. Of course, Debi wanted. So did I.

I went first. When he put the snake on my shoulders, I was surprised how heavy it was. The sheer weight was crushing. I wasn't disappointed when he lifted the snake off.

Debi was next. The soldier put the boa on Debi's slight shoulders. It was at least three times her size and easily could have wrapped around her with less than half its body, yet she lit up with a wide grin.

We were all astonished when Granddad asked to hold the snake. Our grandfather didn't like our cat, bird, coati-mundi, or horse, yet he wanted the huge boa constrictor in his hands? Dad snapped several photos, because Grandma would never believe this either.

From Fort Sherman, we headed to Fort San Lorenzo. The road to the old Spanish fort cut through thick masses of jungle, with a slim view of the ocean once in a while through a break in the bush. For the most part though, we traveled through a dense overgrowth of trees where the double-layered canopy cast seemingly endless shadows on the road.

Margie broke the silence, "I saw something."

Granddad looked up from his newspaper and Debi leaned over him. "What?" she asked.

I was sure she was hoping for a big snake. There were bushmasters out here and she desperately wanted to see one in the wild. That was one experience I could pass on.

"Look!" Margie pointed. "Is that a man coming out of the trees?"

Sure enough, a camouflaged American soldier was stepping out from behind a tree, stopping our car right in the middle of the road.

"Afternoon, sir," he said to Dad through our open car window.

"Good afternoon. Something wrong?"

The soldier made a slight gesture that I almost missed, then several other soldiers, dressed in similar camouflage, stepped out from hiding. They could barely be distinguished from the trees and brushes, they blended so well into the jungle.

"Just want to check your car," the first GI said. "Where are you going?"

"Up to the old fort," Dad said.

The soldier scrutinized each of us. "Anyone else in the car, sir?"

"No."

"Be careful. Don't tell anyone you saw us. Don't pick up anyone. Have a fun trip." His voice was clipped, precise, commanding. Then just like that, all the soldiers vanished into the trees.

"Interesting," Granddad said. "What do you think that was about?"

I still had my eyes glued to the tree line, searching for any human forms. There was no sign that a single person was in that jungle.

"Must be on maneuvers," Dad said as he pressed on the gas pedal to move us on.

Debi said, "Why can't we tell anyone we saw them?"

"It's a game, Debi," Dad answered. "A war game. If we

see other soldiers and tell them we saw the guys down the road, they might lose the game."

That we understood, for we were a game-loving family. The competition was on to spot another soldier. For the rest of the trip to San Lorenzo we focused on the trees. No one won.

The heaviness of the moisture trapped under the umbrella of trees made breathing seem a little harder than usual, until soon the road and the jungle opened to a large clearing with the ocean stretched out ahead of us, bringing a welcoming breeze to dispel the thick jungle smell. I hung out my open window and took long deep breaths of invigorating salty air.

Dad parked by several other cars and we all climbed out. The remains of the impressive old fort proudly stood on the oddly shaped cliff. In its glory days, Spanish soldiers at this key military post had repelled untold attacks from pirates and protected this trail Spaniards had built to transport gold from Peru to Spain.

Directly in front of the fort, the mighty Atlantic's waves crashed onto protruding rocks. Running alongside the cliff was the Chagres River, the same river that flowed to Gamboa miles away, the same river used for commerce and slave trading four hundred years before, the same river pirates had sailed.

Granddad walked with Debi and me to read the engraved metal sign that outlined the history of the fort. In 1502, Christopher Columbus was here. In 1597, the fort was built. Seventy-four years later, Henry Morgan and his band of pirates captured the fort. Over hundreds of years this fort had changed hands through battles of pirates, Spaniards, and the British. This fort had even been part of Colombia at one time. The sign listed facts, but I wished we could know all the stories behind the facts.

No matter how many times Debi and I visited this fort,

we always explored the grounds as if it was our first time. We climbed up and down the vine-covered stone steps. We ventured through openings and in and out of tunnels. We climbed on the cannons anchored to the outer walls centuries before. We crossed the arched bridge that led to the enclosed towers where we had a clear view of the ocean where the Chagres River flowed into it.

Then Debi and I wandered along the bottom level of the fort, which had been a prison at one time. We explored individual cells with manacles still firmly embedded in the masonry. At the end of the corridor, sunlight streamed through massive arching windows to reveal a panoramic vista of the Atlantic Ocean. Another salty breeze drifted into the damp stony dungeon to mingle with the musty air.

Captain Morgan's men had destroyed much of the fort, leaving crevices and stony fractures where bits and pieces of the jungle could encroach. Still, enough of the crumbling fort remained for Debi and me to appreciate how impressive and majestic it once must have been.

Trust Debi to go cautiously poking around corners looking for snakes, both disappointed and relieved when she found none. When we tired of exploring, we crossed the grassy field to the place where Mom had set up our picnic lunch, to find Granddad already there eating a sandwich.

On the drive home, Dad detoured through Gatun and drove down a street with a row of typical Canal Zone residences overlooking the Canal, the houses looking exactly like ours in Gamboa. From the hill, we could see the bridge across the locks and a ship waiting in one of the lock chambers.

"I'm tired, "Margie said. "Let's go."

"This will only take a minute," Dad said. "I want to show your granddad this place. Your sisters, too, because they were too young to remember."

He stopped at one of the houses on the hill. "This house is where we lived the first time we came."

He told us that when he was working for Martin Marietta, he had been sent to the Canal Zone to test the Persian Missile System. He'd rented vacation quarters and we lived in this house for three months.

"Your mom and I would sit in this backyard and watch the ships pass through the locks," he reminisced. "It was during that time, we came to believe the Canal Zone was the place to raise our family. When the job ended, we moved back to the States and I put in an application for a permanent position here. Your mom and I knew we had found our home."

20

The Sunday before Granddad was to leave for home, he came to church with us in Balboa. By the time church let out, my sisters and I were ready to go home, but Mom and Dad had other plans. They wanted to visit a friend in the hospital.

When we complained, Mom said, "We might as well visit him while we're in town."

As we drove down 4th of July Avenue toward Gorgas Hospital, the traffic light turned red and several Panamanian boys appeared with rags and a bucket of water to wash our windshield.

"I don't have any change, do you?" Dad asked Mom. She nodded and Dad told the boys "*Sí, está bien.*" The boys hurriedly splashed water on the windshield so they could finish before the light turned green.

As we waited, a Panamanian woman passed, pushing a younger Panamanian woman in a wheelchair, with visibly crippled legs and several bulging brown packages tied with twine in her lap. Debi and I watched the women jostle along the crowded sidewalk past the *Gran Morrison* department store.

I said, "Wonder what it would be like not to be able to use your legs? Just think, Debi, you could push me around. I'd be riding in style."

Mom said, "I'll bet that woman wishes she had good healthy legs like you girls."

The boys finished wiping our car window and Dad gave

them some change just as the traffic light turned green. Minutes later we were circling the one-level parking garage at the hospital named for Dr. Gorgas.

I said, to no one in particular, "D'you know who Dr. Gorgas is?"

"Yes, Judy," Margie snapped, "you've told us a million times."

"I wasn't talking to you. I was asking Debi."

Before anyone could stop me, I told Debi about the American army doctor from Alabama, credited with reducing the outbreaks of yellow fever and malaria in Panama. One of my schoolteachers had said that was an important factor in the Americans' success in building the Canal, when the French and others had failed.

Children weren't allowed to visit hospital patients, so Margie, Debi, and I had to wait in the car. Only three-year-old Connie, still considered a baby, could go inside. Granddad would stay in the car with us. Dad reminded us we'd better be good because Granddad was too old to tolerate any nonsense.

"It'll only be a few minutes," Mom promised.

The few minutes turned out to be longer than Debi and I could sit still. Margie was engrossed in a book, but Debi and I couldn't stand it anymore.

"We're going to sit on the wall," I told Granddad, who was dozing sitting up. I told Debi that Granddad had nodded his agreement.

The wall surrounding the parking garage wasn't the same height at every point. Following the slope of the hill, at the exit ramp it was only a couple of feet high, then about midway where our van was parked, about five feet high. Higher up, where it met the concrete steps at the front of the hospital, I later learned, that part of the wall was more than fifteen feet high.

To play our game, Debi and I would start at the lower

end and jump off onto the grass on the other side. Then we'd climb back up, walk up the wall a little further and jump again. Whoever could jump from the highest point would win. Simple.

After five minutes of that, we got bored. "Debi," I challenged her, "let's go to the very top and work our way down." That way, I thought, we could decide the winner much sooner. Debi was all for it.

So that time we went and sat on the wall closest to the cement stairs near the front of the hospital, at the wall's highest point. Then I ran down the stairs to see if it looked as high from the bottom of the wall as it did from the top. Actually, it looked higher.

"I'm not jumping from here," Debi said when I came back up. "Let's move down some."

I started to stand up, and before I knew what had happened I was in the air. My feet landed on the grass, but my body crumpled beneath me, shooting excruciating pain up both my legs.

Debi ran down the stairs to me. "Are you okay?"

I managed to sit up, "I don't think I can walk."

She handed me my eyeglasses that had landed a few feet away—thank goodness, they didn't break. "What should I do?"

"Help me up the stairs so I can get in the car. Just don't tell anyone. I don't want Mom mad that we left the car."

So, with Debi's help, I stood up, which made the pain worse. My feet were swelling right out of my sandals. I leaned most of my weight on Debi and hobbled to the stairs, where I sat to take a break. Then still sitting on my rear end, with Debi's help, I pushed myself one step at a time up to the parking level. It took awhile, and Debi and I were both exhausted when we made it, but we managed to shuffle toward the car. It was farther than we thought and we knew Granddad couldn't help us. Margie probably would have helped, but we didn't want to ask her, because she would surely tell on us.

Walking on my heels, I clung to Debi until we managed to get me inside the van, where I crawled behind the seats and lay down in the way back. Margie asked what was wrong, so Debi told her I'd hurt my foot "a little." I was barely settled when Mom and Dad returned.

Dad got behind the wheel, asking, "We good?" He looked at Granddad, who was reading the newspaper by then. Margie and Debi were both reading comic books. "Where's your sister?" Dad said.

"Back here," I called out from behind the seats. "I'm trying to sleep."

Debi kept her eyes glued to the pages of *Archie and Veronica*. As Dad pulled out of the parking garage, I prayed that the pain would go away. I dozed off and on.

When we stopped at Charlie's for fruit and I heard Mom say, "You getting out, Judy?" I pretended to be asleep. Any movement sent a shrilling pain through my feet.

I could hear Debi outside the van, chattering happily to Margie as if nothing had happened. How could she forget me, back here in agony? Would she be buying Chinese plums without me?

Debi was the first one back. She leaned over the back seat and whispered, "I got Chinese plums for us. I won't open the package until we get home and you feel better." Then she turned back around, so Mom wouldn't know I was awake.

The car started up and moved on. After Dad caught the green light at the bridge, I knew it would be only minutes before we got home. I couldn't imagine how I was going to walk from the carport up the stairs to the kitchen, then up the second flight of stairs to my bedroom and pretend everything was okay.

When the rest of the family climbed out of the van, I

didn't move. Dad left the windows rolled down. "She'll be out soon," he told Mom. "She won't be able to stand the heat."

Once everyone was gone, I crawled over the back seat, then, slowly and painfully, tried to walk on my heels, relieved to see that Debi had snuck out the front stairs to help me.

Again, I climbed the steps sitting on my backside. Mom was in the kitchen when we opened the back door.

"What's wrong, Judy? Are you feeling sick?"

"I'll be okay," I said. "For some reason, my feet hurt."

I made it to the living-room couch and collapsed. When Mom came to check on me I reassured her nothing was wrong.

Finally she said, "Your feet don't just start hurting like that for no reason. Let me see them."

Reluctantly, I gave in.

Both my feet were hugely swollen with a purplish color. Unable to keep quiet about it any longer, I told Mom everything.

By now, it was late afternoon. My parents discussed taking me back to Gorgas, even though we all knew that the emergency room at Gorgas on a Sunday evening could mean an all-nighter. It was always best to go first thing in the morning, rested and ready to spend the entire day. Finally the decision was made to wait until the next day, though Mom questioned the wisdom of it. But I didn't feel good and I didn't want to drive back to Gorgas. I certainly didn't want to sit in an emergency room for hours waiting for a doctor. I craved sleep.

Unconvinced, Mom said, "All right. Come get me if you need anything. On second thought, don't move. Send Debi to get me, if you change your mind and want to go to the hospital."

We spent almost the entire next day at Gorgas. The x-ray revealed fractured bones in both my feet. "The wall by the steps?" the doctor asked me, amazed that I'd been able to walk at all. "No more amazing feats for you," he declared.

I came home with thick white plaster casts from my toes to my knees on *both* legs. They reminded me of white Go-Go boots and Dad said I looked quite fashionable. During the three days it would take the plaster to harden I'd have to stay off my feet and after that, walk with my casts on crutches for six weeks.

Friends came over to see for themselves. An hour later, after signing both casts, they all went outside to play. I sat on my bed, reading comic books.

That night Margie came in and played cards with me.

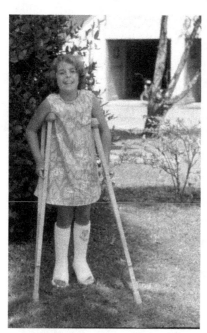

"Do you know what karma is?" she asked.

I shook my head.

"Well, it's because of karma that you have broken legs. You never should've said anything about that woman in the wheelchair."

Judy with her two broken feet

21

T he second year our family was in the Canal Zone, both Mom and Dad took flying lessons. Dad was in love with the idea of being a private pilot of small planes; Mom just wanted to be able to get herself down should Dad have a heart attack in the air. Not that my dad was in bad health—he was very healthy. It's just that Mom was a survivor and in order to survive, you have to know how to take control. She often told us girls, "You cannot let yourself be helpless."

The first time Mom soloed was also the last time she flew alone, although Dad continued the lessons until he certified as a flight instructor. For two years after work, Dad would drive out to Paitilla Airport on the far side of Panama City, fighting city traffic in hopes of getting an hour of flying in before the sun went down. A small Panamanian airport, Paitilla was the only civilian airport available on the Pacific Side to Canal Zone employees. There pilots could choose to land their planes either on the tarmac or on the grassy field.

Dad began to question why Zonians couldn't have their own airstrip. He was told he'd have better luck getting an airstrip approved if he had an incorporated organized club supporting him. So Dad placed a notice on the bulletin board at the Gamboa Clubhouse and another at the Commissary across the street. In no time, interested potential members met and formed the Chagres Aero Club. They were then incorporated by the State of

Delaware and Dad secured a land lease from the Canal Zone government.

Next, Dad had to get authorization from the U.S. military. His persistence paid off. Permission was granted for an airfield in Gamboa. A half mile from the Navy Tank farm, eleven acres of fill dump on the bank of the Canal was designated for a small-engine landing strip. We drove there to celebrate.

After the pavement ended a quarter mile from the field, the dirt road grew considerably narrower, and encroaching untamed jungle weeds scratched at the car. At the place where we parked, a bulky brownish red-backed iguana was sunning lazily on a half-rotten tree limb.

"This," Dad proudly showed us, "will be the parking lot. Over there will be the runway."

When Mom, my sisters, and I looked where he pointed, all we saw was a field of thick-bladed sawgrass, capable of slicing thin gashes on our bare legs. Jungle bordered one side of the field and an overgrown spindly quagmire edging the Canal bordered the other side.

But Dad had a broader vision of galvanized hangars, a singular tower with a pilot office and small airplanes taking off and landing on a soft grassy runway. He sketched plans and wrote notes on his notepad while the rest of us swatted at the invisible insects feasting on our flesh. A few yards away, a steel-gray cargo ship glided through the water, its wake lapping the shore.

On weekends, Dad rented a bulldozer from the Navy Tank farm, the only condition being that their certified operator would run the earthmover. Undeterred, Dad hired him, but when the bulldozer operator went to the Gamboa Golf Club for a three-hour martini lunch, Dad's work ethic couldn't stand it. During those three long hours, he figured out how to operate the bulldozer and bulldozed the field himself. After his lunch, the bleary-eyed operator

Dad bulldozing the Gamboa Airfield at the edge of the Canal

was amazed to see how much more he had accomplished that morning than he had realized!

On some Saturdays, Mom drove us to the field to bring Dad lunch and Debi and I walked down to the banks of the Canal.

"Don't let Connie fall in the water," Mom hollered when our younger sister followed.

"And don't let her get too close to the gators," Dad added.

Debi liked to pick up a large stick for good measure.

In time, it all came together. In 1968, Dad landed a small-engine airplane for the first time at the new Chagres Air Club and soon was flying out of Gamboa every afternoon. One of only a few civilian flight instructors in the Canal Zone, he had more students than he had flying time.

Dad became a partner in a six-seater Cessna and hired himself out to pilot visitors who wanted a bird's-eye view of the Canal Zone. His flying opened the door for him to meet fellow Zonians who also loved to fly, as well as servicemen, international businessmen and dignitaries—even celebrities, including John Wayne.

Dad's flying also opened the door for us daughters to see other parts of Panama. In less than thirty minutes, we could be relaxing and playing on Contadora Island. In the Gulf of Panama on the Pacific Side, *Isla Contadora*, as it's known in Spanish, is a small, irregular, northern part of a chain of islands called *Las Perlas*—Spanish for pearls. Its length from one tip to the other might be a mile and a half. The runway ran almost diagonally at the island's widest part, with a landing strip just a quarter-mile long, but occasionally a plane might slide off into the ocean.

"It's a little tricky," Dad would say just before landing. "Hold your breath, just in case."

When we first started flying out to the island, there was hardly anything there. A few wealthy Panamanians and foreign leaders had weekend homes on one side of the island and a secluded resort was being developed to cater to American celebrities craving privacy. Some trailer homes for construction and maintenance workers were brought in by barge. The island boasted a small bar, a *cantina*, and a restaurant with three or four tables. It was on Contadora Island that the Shah of Iran later came to stay when he was forced into exile.

Once we landed on Contadora, Dad taxied the plane to a side area, where there might be another plane or two. On the beach a few yards from the landing strip, the ocean was quiet and gentle, a welcome contrast to the crashing surf on the mainland of the Pacific Side. Several boats might be anchored in the bay, with the endless horizon stretching behind them like a picture postcard. That isolated beach rarely had more than a handful of people sunbathing on its soft, powdery, crystal-white sand.

In the clear turquoise water, Debi and I snorkeled and tried to catch colorful fish with our hands. Back in the 1500s, these islands had been the home of pearl divers, and the name *Contadora* means "counting house," as that was where the divers brought their pearls to be counted and inventoried before they were shipped to Spain.

Debi and I searched in vain for missed pearls, hoping we could have our own house on this beautiful *isla*. Out of the millions of people living on the earth, relatively few people have known about this place. We were two of the lucky ones and we knew it.

After several hours, we climbed back into the plane. Debi and Connie squeezed into the far back two seats. Most of the time when we flew, I sat directly behind Dad in one of the two middle seats. Margie usually sat beside me. We each had our own side window, but the windows in the far back were much smaller.

"Do you see the sharks?" Margie asked, seconds after the plane took off. I strained to see the ocean below. The water was crystal clear, but I couldn't see any sharks.

Debi perked up in the back seat, "Where?"

Margie pointed out her window, "Right there."

"You can't see them from your side," Dad hollered back over the engine noise.

Debi practically crawled over Connie to look out Margie's window to see the sharks. Connie cried out, telling Debi to get back to her side of the plane. Debi ignored her.

"How big are they?" Debi asked.

Margie sat smugly back in her seat. "They're gone now. You missed them."

Disappointed, Debi settled back in her seat, and before she could even sigh, we felt the plane turn. I smiled. Dad was flying us back to see the sharks.

Margie groaned impatiently. "Oh, let's go."

Dad turned a wide enough circle so the sharks would be on Debi's and my side of the plane, took us down a little lower, and there were the large dark shapes beneath the surface of the crystal-clear sea below.

Suddenly I tensed. The sharks swam just a few feet from where Debi and I had been blissfully snorkeling, in our personal paradise.

Armbruster girls (and Mom) in life jackets aboard ship

The pool on the S. S. Cristobal

22

Every other year Dad had to declare his intentions to renew his contract with his company and finalize our summer travel arrangements. Canal Zone workers got home leave to return to the States for a few weeks, and the contract included transportation for the entire family.

We had several options. Sometimes, along with other Canal Zone workers, we flew to and from Miami on a chartered Pan Am or Braniff plane. The two-hour flight was a social event, as Zonians frequently switched seats throughout the flight, chatting with friends and neighbors.

Twice we drove up through Central America and entered the States through Texas. On two other occasions we drove home to Panama from Florida. All those car trips were grueling. Sometimes because we'd even have to clear rocks and other debris off the Central American roads, so we always packed our van with fresh drinking water and cans of Hi-C to last through six countries. Our overnight stops were in shabby hotels reminiscent of bad Western movies.

By far, our favorite way to travel was on the *S.S. Cristobal*, a ship owned by the Panama Canal Company. When we went that way, for three days we cruised with about two hundred other Zonians, enjoying the almost constant party atmosphere. We celebrated going to the States and we celebrated going home to Panama.

In preparation for one of those summer vacations to the States, Dad called us down from our bedrooms for a family meeting. A large U.S. map lay spread out on the kitchen table. That year Dad had two months of vacation. Where did we want to go?

In less than two hours, we all agreed. We'd take the *Cristobal* up to the States. At New Orleans, we'd buy a new VW van. First, we'd drive to California, stop at Disneyland, and continue up the coast to Washington State, then over to Salt Lake City and Wyoming where we'd visit Yellowstone National Park, the Badlands, Mt. Rushmore, and Indian reservations, and for our last month, we'd end up at Grandma's house in Florida.

Dad pulled out his thick address book of his many military friends who were once stationed in Panama and now lived in the States. Often they would invite us to spend a night or two in their homes and show us local sights in their communities. On nights when we weren't invited to stay with anyone, we'd camp in our new VW camper at state parks.

With our summer trip organized, Debi and I went to bed excited. We talked about Disneyland and camping at Yellowstone National Park. We would stay with Julia's family in Colorado, where her father was now stationed, and visit the Air Force Academy. In Kentucky, we'd stay with cousins on their farm outside of Lexington. We'd even get to travel home on the ship.

I commented that we wouldn't get home until two days before school started.

Debi said, "What did you say?"

"I said, it'll be fun to stay in the States until right before school. Just think, we'll come home, and two days later we'll be back in school."

"That's not fair!"

Without another word, she stormed downstairs. Sound carried in our house, so from upstairs I could hear Debi explaining to Mom and Dad that she was tired of missing her birthday.

"Why did I have to be born in August?" she demanded. I didn't hear their answers.

Even when it wasn't for home leave, we went to the States in July and stayed through most of August. During non–home-leave years, the Panama Canal Company didn't pay a travel allowance, so we'd stay at Grandma's and not take a road trip. The one summer when we didn't leave the Canal Zone, Debi still didn't have a birthday party, because her friends were all away on home leave and there was no one around to invite.

She came back upstairs and flopped on her bed, moaning that I didn't understand. *My* birthday was in September. It was always remembered. At school, people told me, "Happy Birthday." Sometimes I had a party and my friends would all come. At church, I always got recognized for being a year older.

"Debi …" I said, getting out of bed to turn out the light.

"I don't want to talk," she mumbled, her voice thick as if she was swallowing tears.

I lay there in the dark, unable to sleep. Every fifteen or twenty minutes, our bedroom window would rattle and vibrate from ships passing through the Canal. I would watch the small beacon of light from the ship's high mast start at the corner of the wall that faced my bed and travel across to the other corner. Once the light passed through my room I heard the window in Connie's room rattle and knew that the same beacon of light was shining on her bedroom wall. This pattern would follow to my parents' room, then to the small, added bedroom where Margie slept before continuing to the next house.

Another ship came by and another small round light floated on my wall as the windows shook softly. I don't know how many ships passed by before I finally fell asleep.

The next day, Debi beat me home from school. She must have left right after school without stopping to talk to her friends. On her bed were torn pages of a calendar, spread out so that each month was visible. With a pencil sticking out of her mouth, she was concentrating on the pages.

"What do you think about January 20th?" she asked.

"For what?"

"My new birthday."

"What are you talking about?"

"Well, September is your birthday. October is Halloween. November is Thanksgiving. December is Christmas. February is Valentine's Day. March is Easter. April is Connie's birthday, and May is the end of school. That only leaves January."

I found a t-shirt and a pair of shorts. "You can't change your birthday."

"Why not?"

"Because you have a birth certificate. That tells you and the whole world the day you were born."

"Doesn't matter. My Sunday School teacher said that December 25th isn't really the birthday of Jesus. She said we just celebrate it that day. I am now going to celebrate my birthday on January 20th." She ran downstairs to tell Mom.

Sure enough, Debi had her birthday party on January 20th, five months after her actual birthday. Mom decorated the patio underneath the house with streamers and balloons, and we hung a colorful donkey piñata from one of the floor joists. We had a Barbie Doll cake, of course, and punch, and played games and Debi got lots of presents.

Later that month Debi and I came home from school to find the dining-room table covered with a party tablecloth. A decorated cake sat in the middle, and presents were stacked on a side table.

"You girls go upstairs," Mom said. "This is for a baby shower."

I started walking up the stairs. "Can't I at least have some cake?" I whined.

"Afterward, if there's any left. For now, go play in your room."

Debi and I changed clothes and lay on our beds, reading a new stack of traded comic books. The noise and fun drifted up from downstairs until finally Debi couldn't stand it any more. She tiptoed to the stairs and crept down a few steps to peer between the balusters taking everything in, then tiptoed back to our room.

"It must be fun having a baby," she said. "Just think, in one year, Mrs. Taylor can have birthday presents, Christmas presents, and baby presents. That's three times in one year she'll get presents." She picked up the box of fish food and sprinkled droplets in the round fishbowl. "I've got it, Judy. I'm having a baby shower."

"How are you going to do that? You're not having a baby."

Debi peered intently through the glass bowl and admired her guppy's swollen belly. The dark spot by the tail was a tiny bit bigger than yesterday. "I'm not, but my fish is. I don't know when, but soon."

Debi went to Mom's room and came back with construction paper and scissors. With broken crayons, she made eight baby-shower invitations. On a piece of notebook paper, she planned her party for Saturday.

"Do you have any money?" she asked me.

"Some." I took my piggy bank out of my drawer and counted out sixty cents. Debi had thirty. Enough to buy some candy.

Once Mom's guests left our house, Debi and I went downstairs and ate a piece of cake. We carefully took down the baby-shower decorations and folded each one to match the creases. If Mom was surprised at our unusual helpfulness she didn't say so.

I checked the pantry, found a brownie mix on the shelf, and hid it. I didn't want anyone making the brownies yet. We'd need them for the guppy baby shower.

Saturday afternoon, Debi and I decorated the underneath of our house for the shower. I covered the table with the baby-shower tablecloth and then put the pan with the baked brownies on top. I laid the little cardboard cutout of a baby rattle on top of the pan of brownies, like I'd seen on the other cake. Debi and I set out little bowls with pieces of candy we'd bought with our change, and we mixed a pitcher of Kool-Aid, which we poured into the left-over baby-shower paper cups.

Debi's friends showed up with small packages wrapped in napkins, notebook paper, and old Christmas wrap. We played traditional baby-shower games, then Debi unwrapped the gifts.

Graciously, she thanked her friends for the half-empty box of fish food from someone else's supply, a used comic book to read to the new babies, a ring that came from a box of Cracker Jacks to commemorate the birth, and a tiny, old, faded, plastic scuba diver to decorate the nursery.

After the guests left, Debi packed all the gifts in a shoe box, and we went back upstairs. When I opened the kitchen door, our parrot Harry called, "Come in." We ignored him and he gave us a long wolf whistle. We ignored that, too, and walked on upstairs to our bedroom where we sat on our beds talking about the guppy shower and how much fun it was, completely forgetting what a mess we'd left behind. That didn't bother us. Maria would take care of it for us. She always did.

23

Our two months of summer vacation in the States passed quickly. Dad arranged to bring Grandma back with us to spend three weeks in Panama, while Granddad took care of things in Florida. She had visited us several times in the past, but this was her first time coming by ship.

After our month at Grandma's, we arrived back in New Orleans a day early, so we could get the VW van loaded onto the *Cristobal*, as cargo going to the Canal Zone had to be loaded the day before the passengers. As soon as we checked into two rooms at the Holiday Inn on Canal Street, Debi turned on the TV.

"Is that all you girls think about?" Grandma said. "You'll rot your brains out." We did watch a lot of TV at Grandma's house, but we tried to explain to her that we only had one English television channel in Panama, which never had the shows available in the States. We wanted to watch as many summer reruns as we could squeeze in, between Grandma's soap operas and the chores required of us.

There were still episodes of *Gilligan's Island, Batman,* and *I Dream of Jeannie* that we hadn't seen and in addition, we wanted to finish memorizing the jingles on the commercials, so we could sing them to our friends who weren't going to the States that year. Commercials weren't shown on Armed Forces television stations either and our friends always did the same for us.

"While we're here, let's walk down to the French Quarter and explore Bourbon Street," Dad suggested.

"Ah, c'mon, Dad," Debi and I whined. "This is our last night of TV."

Grandma and Dad shared a love of history, but she wasn't sold on the idea of going to the street of iniquity. Dad convinced her that not all the streets in the French Quarter had a reputation and it was still daylight. The real sins didn't happen until after dark set in. Grandma relented and picked up her purse.

"Let's go, girls," Dad said. "You never know when you'll get another opportunity to see these sights." He was big on not missing anything. "Cram in as much living as you can," he said, "because you never know when things are going to change."

Dad, Grandma, Mom, and we four girls made our way through the historic streets of New Orleans, as Connie, now four, was able to do more with us. We marveled at the beautiful French architecture and scenic courtyards, joked at the comical gargoyles and whimsical fountains.

"If these walls could talk ..." Grandma mused aloud several times, "what they would tell us."

The last street we turned down was Bourbon Street. "We'll just walk a block or two," Dad said to his mother. By now, darkness was beginning to set in and tourists and sightseers were crowding the street.

I saw Grandma's back stiffen. "I'll walk the way we came," she said.

"Don't be silly," Dad said. "That way's much longer, and it's getting dark."

She wouldn't budge.

"Look," he continued, "it's just two short blocks. We turn that corner and we're almost at the hotel. We'll walk fast."

She relented, pursed her lips, and steeled herself to

walk down the infamous street.

An interesting mixture of people and the clothes they were wearing caught Debi's and my attention. She could zero in on the funniest things, cracking us both up in fits of giggles. Margie walked her standard ten paces in front of the family. She wanted no part of her obviously immature sisters. Mom held onto Connie's hand. Grandma reminded Dad once more that this might not be the best street for his four young daughters to be walking down. It was her duty to make sure that Mom and Dad brought their daughters up with the best moral standards.

When Debi noticed a half-naked girl swinging out of a second-story window on a swing like a child's, she poked me in the side to get my attention.

"That looks like fun!" Debi exclaimed, a little too loudly. Grandma and Dad both turned to see what she was talking about.

"Dad, I want to do that!" Debi pleaded. Grandma went pale.

"No, Debi." Dad tried to divert her attention. "C'mon over here."

"Wait a minute," Debi responded impatiently. "I'm watching this." The girl was swinging back and forth through the window. "It's kind of like a cuckoo clock, with a door opening and a girl coming out. Look at that!"

"I see it, Debi. Come on," Dad urged.

Debi started walking, but kept looking back at the swing. "When I grow up, Dad, that's going to be my job. It would be so much fun to swing in and out of a window."

I stopped to look back at the window again, too, until I felt Grandma's hard finger on my shoulder, firmly nudging me to keep walking. At any minute, she would start reciting Bible verses and we all knew it.

"Let's go in this store," Mom spoke up, partly to distract us, partly because curiosity and novelty shops always fascinate her. So Mom entered the dingy souvenir shop, to find it filled with pewter chalices, small sculptured stoneware, and hanging t-shirts. The rest of us dutifully followed her inside.

Holding Connie's hand, Mom went over to the jewelry counter, while Margie, Debi, and I were drawn to the rows and rows of touristy t-shirts in the back of the store. Debi picked out one with an obnoxious phrase on it and started giggling.

A man in loose-fitting faded blue jeans and a black t-shirt zeroed in. "Want that shirt?" he said.

Debi hung the shirt back on the rack. "I was just looking at it."

"I'm serious," he said. "I want your shirt. I'll trade your shirt for any other shirt in this store."

By then, Grandma was standing right next to us. She grabbed Debi and glared at the stranger. "I. Beg. Your.

*The van being loaded on the S.S. Cristobal
in New Orleans*

Pardon." She stressed each word strongly, with precision. The beginning of a commotion brought over Mom and Dad as well.

The man in the black t-shirt smiled. "Didn't mean to scare you. This is my store. I happened to notice your granddaughter's shirt. It's unusual. I'd like to buy it."

We all looked at Debi's shirt as if it was the first time we'd seen it—her old *mola* shirt made by the Cuna Indians in Panama. It was worn out, fraying at the seams.

"This is my favorite shirt," Debi said truthfully.

"I'm willing to trade you for any shirt in the store. You pick out a shirt, change in the dressing room, and give me your old shirt. Then you'll have a brand-new shirt."

Dad, sensing a deal, said, "Sir, that shirt comes from Panama. The Indians down there make those shirts by hand. They're kind of hard to come by."

I didn't say a thing, but I knew darn well we could get shirts like Debi's any day of the week. Dad made it sound like it was rare.

"Okay," the store owner conceded. "I'll throw in twenty dollars."

Dad paused for a dramatic minute, then reluctantly agreed.

Debi said, "Don't I get to say anything? It's *my* shirt."

"Just think, Debi, you'll get a brand-new shirt." I urged her.

"So?"

The store owner casually walked to the cash register. "Let me know what you decide."

Dad promised Debi he'd get her another *mola* shirt, too. That meant she'd end up with two new shirts, so she agreed. The shirt was getting too small for her anyway. Debi went to change, and the owner gave my dad a $20 bill.

I didn't think it was fair that Debi got two new shirts and I didn't get anything, so Dad said I could pick out a t-shirt. Margie wanted one, too. And Connie. Mom threw in a pair of earrings, and Grandma, minty Life Savers.

Dad handed the store owner the $20 back and reached for his wallet to pay the difference.

"You girls sure know how to ruin a man's good deal," he said as we walked back to the hotel.

The next morning, we four Armbruster girls boarded the *S.S. Cristobal* wearing our brand-new shirts with "New Orleans" spelled out in large glaring letters.

24

E ager to see our stateroom, Debi and I followed Mom and Grandma down the crowded corridor. On the trip up to the States, we'd been assigned two adjoining staterooms, the standard boring type with two metal bunks welded to cement walls and nothing more. Not exciting at all.

This time our family had a suite. The door opened up to a small sitting room, a couch and two overstuffed chairs taking up most of the space. A small glass window gave us an ocean view.

On either side of the main room were staterooms with two sets of bunk beds anchored to the steel walls. Debi and I each claimed the top bunks. Margie tossed her purse on the bunk under Debi's. Connie would sleep under my bed.

More than satisfied with our quarters, Debi and I went back up on deck to watch people board, hoping we'd see someone we knew walk up the ramp. If we did, not only would we have someone to do things with onboard, we could tell them all about our vacation.

Within minutes, Debi saw one of her friends with her family, checking in with the steward.

"Susan, Susan!" Debi yelled, waving like a maniac. Susan looked up and waved back. Debi squeezed through the mass of people to speak to her, then ran back to me. "Remember this number," she told me and repeated the number. "That's Susan's stateroom. I gave her our number, too."

Before I knew it, Debi was making her way through

the crowd again, because two more of her friends were boarding.

I studied the line of people, hoping I wouldn't be left with no friends on the trip home. Margie had found a few of her friends, and they were already in the lounge talking.

Then Debi was back by my side with a huge smile. Three friends! They'd planned to meet at the pool after the standard life-jacket emergency drill.

Once the ship was officially boarded, a voice over the loudspeakers announced we were ready to sail.

"All ashore that's going ashore!"

The *S.S. Cristobal* had one small pool, two ping-pong tables, a shuffle-board court, and wooden-slatted deck chairs. Our family was assigned two deck chairs outside our cabin window. Inside, the ship had a main lounge downstairs, with a grand staircase leading up to a smaller lounge with a small TV screen suspended from the ceiling. Down a narrow corridor were a library and a sitting room. On the last night of the cruise, the main lounge was always transformed with chairs and a wide movie screen, to allow families to celebrate the last night at sea watching a movie together.

Debi and I ran up to the top deck and stood by the railings at the ship's bow. We could see the division between the ocean's distinct blue and the muck-brown Mississippi River current through which our ship was gliding. Dad had told us that he had swum in the Mississippi River when he was a boy, a thought that disgusted Debi and me. That brownish water was nothing like the tropical blue sea we always got to swim in on Panama's beaches.

As the ship nosed closer to the Gulf of Mexico, Debi and I ran to the stern, because once we left the dirty water, we were no longer in the United States. Though we would miss many things about being in the States, we were more than happy to be going home.

The voice over the loudspeaker announced that all the passengers had to assemble for the mandatory safety drill. Debi and I rushed to our stateroom and struggled into bulky orange vests. Between trying to find our sea legs and being top-heavy with the heavily padded life jackets, we waddled on deck to find our assigned place in the jam-packed line of life-jacketed passengers. There we had to stand so long, our legs hurt while the steward explained the life-saving procedures.

"Judy," Debi whispered, "remember in the cartoon where the two fat guys bump stomachs and go *Boiiing*?"

I nodded, knowing where this was going.

"We could do that now."

"I don't think that's a good idea, Debi. What if we fall?"

She started to crack up. "It would be like dominoes."

When she nudged me with her life jacket, I teetered off balance and grabbed onto Margie in front of me. She grabbed onto Mom, who was holding Connie's shoulders to keep her steady and quiet. Both Mom and Margie shot me an angry look. I hissed at Debi, who flashed me a huge mischievous grin.

"I'm not playing, Debi," I said in my most serious tone.

Then she undertook to tie the straps of her life vest together. I hoped she'd make a big knot and be stuck in her hot life jacket for the rest of the trip. I hoped they'd have to cut off the straps to get her out and she'd have to pay for a new one with her allowance.

Finally the horn blew for the end of our safety exercise. At last we could leave. Debi and I tore off our life jackets, handed them to Mom, and begged her to put them away for us.

"You girls take care of that yourself," Grandma cut in. "Can't you see that your mom has enough to do with your little sister? You should be helping her, not asking her to help you."

Privately, I knew this would be a long few weeks with Grandma visiting.

Eventually the passengers settled in and peacefulness came over the ship. I left Debi and her friends on the top deck watching the empty swimming pool fill with ocean water. Debi was determined to be one of the first into the pool, once the workers unlocked the chain and pronounced it open. Mom, Grandma, and Connie sat in our assigned lounge chairs and watched for whales. Margie was nowhere to be found. I walked the corridors and lounges hoping to find one of my friends, but saw no one I knew. This had never happened to me on our other trips. Trying not to feel sorry for myself, I leaned against the steel deck railings and peered out at the sea. Maybe I would spot my own whale.

I heard a voice next to me, "Hi. Name is Rhoda."

Rhoda was about my age, with long, straight, blond hair and freckles dotting her face, "I live in Gatun."

I told her my name and that I lived on the other side, in Gamboa.

She shrugged, "Oh. Wanna play cards?"

We headed to the upstairs lounge and asked the steward for a deck of cards. At a table, we began with, "Go Fish," then "War," and finished with "Crazy Eights." We played until dinnertime. My family had the first service for meals—hers had the second. It would be late by the time her family finished dinner.

The next morning when I got to the lounge, I found Rhoda sitting with a couple of older kids playing poker with a large pile of pennies in front of her. She began teaching me the ins and outs of poker and gave me ten pennies. Before long, I was winning a little, but losing more. My pennies didn't last long. I ran downstairs to our stateroom and opened the top dresser drawer where Mom kept change for us to buy an occasional lemonade or soda.

I grabbed a small handful, stuffed the coins in my shorts pockets, and hurried back upstairs. Rhoda was still playing with the same group of kids. I sat back down.

At some point I managed to accumulate my own growing pile of coins and even gave Rhoda some when she ran low. Once we depleted all the change from the group, we joined a couple of men at a larger table who were also playing penny poker. I quit after I lost the first hand, realizing that these guys were much more experienced.

Both of my pockets were full of change when I opened the stateroom door. Grandma, sitting on the couch looking out at the ocean, said she had spotted some flying fish. I opened the dresser drawer and emptied most of my pockets.

Grandma turned and faced me. "What are you doing?"

"Putting money back in the drawer."

"That's a lot of change. Where did you get it?"

"I won it."

"You what?" Her voice rose a little bit.

I wasn't sure what the problem was, "I won it playing poker."

Mom, hearing the exchange, came of out of one of the smaller staterooms and Debi came out of the other.

"Hey," Debi said, "I want to learn to play." She had seen all the change in the drawer.

"Okay, I'll be playing again later this afternoon. You can come if you want. Then we can play poker when we get home."

The look Grandma gave Mom was the only signal Debi and I needed to get out quick.

"Debi, want to go to the bar with me and get Shirley Temples?"

Grandma got to her feet, "Go *where*?"

"Not in the bar, Grandma," I said. "They don't let kids inside the bar. There's a window outside for us kids."

Debi couldn't leave it there, though. "*I* went inside the bar," she said, shocking us all.

"How did you get in?" Mom's voice was steady, but I could tell she wasn't pleased.

"I just followed a bunch of men and walked in with them."

I was impressed, "You're kidding me. What'd you see?"

Grandma tried to freeze Debi with a hard look and Mom shook her head.

"Oh, I didn't see much. It was pretty dark. As soon as I got in, the bartender said I had to leave."

It seemed the more we said, the more upset Grandma got.

Mom said, "Get lemonade, girls, not Shirley Temples."

"Fine by us." At that point, we'd have agreed to anything to get out of the stateroom. I hadn't even touched the door handle before Grandma was telling Mom, "I guess you know two of your girls are on the road to bad news." Knowing that Grandma was probably going to start reading to Mom from her Bible, Debi and I cleared out, though we felt bad for getting Mom in trouble

We stood on the deck holding our paper cups of lemonade and watching a ping-pong game. Sometimes a player hit the ball so hard that the other player missed and the ball flew right off the ship. Usually by the end of the second day at sea, all the ping-pong balls would be gone, leaving this corner of the ship quiet.

By Day Two of our trip we'd run out of things to do. Debi and her friends had already shared their summer vacation stories and there was nothing new to say. Tomorrow night would be movie night and the day after that, we would dock. Until then, long hours stretched before us.

25

"Take your arm out of the water," Dad told me. "You're causing a drag. Besides, you don't know what's in the water. You could run your hand right over the back of a crocodile and wake him up."

That was all I needed to make me take my arm out of the water.

Dad was taking Grandma and me with his crew to Candelaria, one of his field sites. The canal locks are powered by the water flow and part of Dad's job was to accurately measure, collect, and report the river depth and speed of the water current as it passed the various field stations on the rainforest's different rivers.

Maintaining the levels of the manmade lakes was vital, for if the water was too high, the gates of Madden Dam would be opened and the locks would flood out. If the water was too low, ships couldn't carry as much cargo through the locks. They would have to unload some cargo to be taken by train to the Other Side, where it would be reloaded onto the ship.

To get to Candelaria, we rode in a *cayuco*—an open boat carved from a tree trunk. These dugouts sit low in the water and are bigger than a canoe. Some small *cayucos* hold only three or four people, while others are large enough to hold fifteen or twenty people with ease. *Cayucos* also can be powered by motor.

Our *cayuco* had a prop-driven motor, which got us quickly across the river's mouth. Where the river narrowed, we stopped for the crewman to change to a jet-output motor more appropriate for shallow curves and rapids. The hydrographic substations were midway between the river's mouth and the headwaters.

One crewman stood at the front of the boat with a long pole called a *palonca,* which he moved from side to side checking for long tree branches and other debris that might damage the boat. At some points, the river was very narrow and the ever present jungle laid a claustrophobic heaviness over the air. Grandma scanned the river bank, taking in our overall surroundings, as Dad kept his .410 double-barreled pistol handy, in case a snake or a panther got too curious.

We reached the job site and climbed out of the *cayuco* onto a wooden dock. A couple of Panamanian crew workers used their *machetes* to slash away some of the jungle grass that had crept over the walkway to the two-story wooden substation housing the equipment for measuring rain and water flow. Their strong determined *machete* strokes cleared the overgrowth far better than any lawnmower could do.

Vibrant green plants of all shapes and sizes occupied every available space. Some grew on top of each other, vying for precious sunlight. Beyond that, the jungle was alive with the din of birds, monkeys, insects, and other peculiar voices. I found it both thrilling and unsettling.

"Grandma," I said, walking beside her, "we might be the only human beings around, but we aren't alone. The trouble is, you can't see what's keeping us company."

Grandma's answer was characteristic, "Judy, I hope you're living right."

Sometimes Dad and his crew had to stay a few days at this work station to collect all the information he needed. Inside the substation were a couple of cots and an old couch, with a small kitchen in the corner, and nothing more than a radio and other electronic equipment.

I was more than ready to leave by the time we climbed back into the *cayuco*. On the return trip, I sat in the middle of the boat behind Grandma, knowing it didn't rock as much there. That way, if something should jump in the boat with us, I had people in front of me and people behind me.

Slowly we headed back down the river. Rivers are the roads of the jungle and a slight turn can take you somewhere you didn't intend to go. A slight turn that day took us to the tribe of Choco Indians, who live along the banks of the river. That time of year, the river was low, so the boat stopped at a big longitudinally sliced calabash tree trunk. It reminded me of the balance beam at our gym, except it was about two-and-half times longer and had been notched with a *machete* to provide footholds. There was no dock, so the crewman secured the *cayuco* by lashing a rope around the beam. We stepped off the boat and balanced our way on the beam to the embankment.

A couple of women squatted on rocks in the river washing clothes. Their bare breasts drooped heavily and their copper-colored skin was intricately painted over their lower face and other parts of their bodies. They raised their heads and gave us shy smiles, then looked at each other, giggled, and chattered in a language I didn't know.

Grandma smiled back at them and when she and I stepped off the beam, a crowd of these natives surrounded us. They were living a natural life in the jungle, as their people had done for generations. I felt as if I had stepped into the pages of the *National Geographic* magazines we received at home in the mail.

The Choco men wore only a Tarzan-type g-string cloth and earrings. The Choco women wore only a colorful one-piece sarong tied around the waist and ending at their knees. A few of both sexes wore necklaces of a sort, and

Grandma visiting the Choco (now called Emberi) Indians

San Blas Indian woman

Judy and Choco (Emberi) Indian girl

Choco village tucked in the jungle upriver

all had straight black hair. Clearly they loved beauty, for they expressed it through their vivid body paint, fabrics, and ornaments.

Privately, I wondered what Grandma thought of this crowd of half-naked people, who were clearly drawn to her. Four feet nine inches tall, she was the same height as many of the primitive women. I doubted if any of them had ever seen an old white woman with short, curly, white hair. It was obvious to all of us that she made an impression on them.

In a few moments the Indian women circled Grandma, touched her skin, and cooed with delight and curiosity. They were quick to laugh and showed no awkwardness. In turn, Grandma laughed and touched their skins, admiring their heavily painted bodies. She nodded approvingly at their babies and gave indications of appreciating the baskets some of the women were weaving. If Grandma was the least bit uncomfortable, she didn't show it. Only her white hair and American sleeveless dress set her apart from the happy sisterhood of women who surrounded her.

Each family of the Choco lived on a platform raised on stilts. Roosters and chicken ran freely under their homes. Their shelter had no walls, only a thatched roof to keep out sun and rain. Poles framed the roof where the hammocks were tied for beds. Everything they owned was out in the open and visible. To reach their houses, each family used a crude ladder in the form of a cut piece of timber. One side of the poles, like the one at the river landing, had carved notches serving as steps.

Dad warned me that it was rude to look into their homes and said that when the family didn't want guests to come into their homes, they turned the pole-like ladder smooth side outward.

"There's the chief," Dad said, waving in greeting to a man who was walking the dirt path toward us.

There could be no question that this man was in charge. Chief Tony was an inch taller than five feet. Like the other small muscular people of his tribe, his body was generously coated with body paint, which I later learned was made from a native berry. Unlike the other tribesmen, he had an imposing air of authority that would not be challenged, though he was not the least bit solemn. His broad face carried an equally broad smile. Like his tribe members, he was quick to laugh and his eyes lit up. A green parrot on his shoulder was imitating the chief, which amused him.

Dad and Chief Tony were friends. Dad told me the chief was a master of jungle survival. As an adult, he had learned to speak fluent Spanish and a few English words. He had taught astronauts, airmen, and Special Forces teams how to survive in a jungle environment, including how to use native plants for medicinal purposes.

It was the Choco Indians' native root remedies that had saved my dad's boss, Frank Robinson, after a fer-de-lance snake bit him. This pit viper is the most dangerous snake in Panama and one of the deadliest snakes in the world. Without proper medical intervention, its venom can kill a man in less than forty-five minutes.

Later, gliding toward home in the *cayuco* through the almost still river, I listened to the eerie concatenation of jungle noises. It seemed a magical time and place. I was part of something that most people would never know. All too soon we would change motors and be whisked back to cement and manicured yards.

26

E ver since Debi's shirt was bought off her back in New Orleans, she'd been pestering Dad for a new *mola* shirt and Grandma was all for flying out to San Blas as well. On a Saturday morning, I got up early to go with them. Mom and Maria were planning to do their monthly washing-down of the walls to stave off mildew, so I didn't want to be home. Margie had already gone to the stables. I hurriedly beat everyone else to the bathroom to be sure I had time to eat breakfast.

I poured cereal into my bowl and checked to make sure there were no bugs in the flakes. I chose Rice Krispies, because it's the easiest for spotting the tiny vermin and I was in a hurry. Seconds later, Debi came down and poured herself a bowl of Rice Krispies and searched for bugs, while I grabbed the sugar out of the freezer. It took several years of living in the Canal Zone to teach us the only way to keep bugs out of the flour and sugar was to keep those items in the freezer. Before that, whenever we made Kool-Aid, we had to spend long minutes tediously picking the minuscule black beads from the white sugar crystals. Any we missed floated to the top of the Kool-Aid, so I'd have to dip them out with a spoon. Grape Kool-Aid was too dark to spot them, so you drank that flavor at your peril.

At the Gamboa airfield, Dad had reserved the club's four-seater plane, so Debi and I climbed into the back where we each had a narrow triangular seat by a window. Grandma settled in the front seat and reminded us to put

on our seatbelts and Dad called out, "Clear," before he
started the propeller.

Debi asked Dad why he yelled, "Clear," when the only
people at the airfield were sitting inside the plane.

"It's a rule of flying, Debi."

"No one would know," she said. "There's nobody else
here."

"I would know."

Our first stop was Paitilla Airfield for fuel and for a
Zarpee—permission to fly in Panamanian airspace and to
land at any other civilian airports.

Thirty minutes later, we landed on *Islanda Aligondí* in
the San Blas Islands, home of the Kuna Indians. Like the
Chocos, these people also had preserved their culture and
remained independent from Panama—a country within a
country, with its own customs and laws.

Because the islands have no source of fresh water, the
Kuna people hauled water from the mainland in motor-
ized *Cayucos* or captured rain in barrels behind huts.
Dozens of grass huts crowded the island about the size of
a football field. The huts, made from bamboo and palm
fronds, had walls for privacy, but we could see through
the open doors. Hammocks hung neatly from the bamboo framing, and we could see tiny lines scratched in the
dirt floor from brooms. It seemed odd to me that anyone
would sweep a dirt floor clean.

The minute we started to walk through the village, a
crowd of curious children surrounded us. "Remember,"
Dad reminded us, "don't let anyone give you a baby to
hold. And don't take a child's hand." Grandma tucked her
hands into her dress pockets.

There was a very good reason why we couldn't do this.
Most people might think it strange that a mother would
offer a foreigner her child to hold, then scurry off to a
hidden part of the island, leaving the foreigner and child

alone, both desperate to find her. I thought it was weird until Dad explained that the mothers wanted their children to be reared by Americans to give them a better quality of life. It was hard to pretend not to notice the children and focus instead on why we were here—to get *molas* and lobsters.

Molas are part of the traditional costume worn by Kuna girls and women. Each blouse has a *mola* design on the front and the back, with sleeves and backing made of ordinary cotton cloth. The bottom of the costume is a long cotton skirt. The women also adorn themselves with strands of glass beads that they wrap tightly around their forearms and calves. They cover their heads with a red-and-orange scarf, some allowing a bit of their jet-black hair to peek out from under the scarf. All Kunas have eyes that are darker than midnight.

We stopped at hut after hut, inviting the women to show us their *molas*. Grandma and Dad were very picky. Dad told us that a few years ago, when a Kuna chief was traveling on the mainland, he learned of pedal-powered sewing machines and brought them to the island, so that now many Kunas used them to make their *molas*. But Dad only wanted hand-stitched ones. Grandma also inspected each one for any signs of fraying and fading, while Debi just concentrated on finding a new shirt.

Like the Choco Indians, the Kuna people are tiny and short-statured. I had learned in school that the only people smaller than the Kunas were pygmies. Their shirts were no longer big enough for me, so I settled for smaller-sized *molas* to sew as patches on my jeans. Grandma was picking a few gifts for friends and Dad wanted some worthy of framing.

So many women were bringing out their *molas* and urging us to buy from them that I hated to choose. Every time I got close to picking one, another Indian woman would touch my arm and show me her stack of *molas* to finger. Kunas have their own language and don't speak English, though a few of the men speak Spanish. Our bartering came down then to pantomime and sign language, but that didn't mean we got away with anything. Mom always said that the Kuna women are some of the sharpest businesswomen she ever knew. They might need our American dollars, but they knew how to deal.

So did Dad. He would put some *molas* in a pile and show a couple of dollars. The women would shake their heads meaning "No." He would take some larger pieces off and throw on some smaller ones. The women would chatter among themselves, then one of them would replace a very colorful *mola* with a not-so-colorful *mola* and nod for, "Yes." Dad would shake his head, "No," remove the not-so-colorful *mola*, and offer less money. This would lead to another Kuna woman adding a piece of her handiwork and pointing to Dad to put more money down. The pantomime seemed to have no end.

Grandma thought it was fascinating and sometimes got in the act with Dad, but Debi and I grew bored. Finally though, an agreement was made.

Buying the lobsters was not nearly such an ordeal. Lobsters went for twenty-five cents apiece regardless of weight, and some lobsters easily weighed two or three pounds. Dad had Kuna men pile the lobsters in his burlap sack, and we loaded them onto the plane.

After we got home, Dad emptied the sack of live lobsters onto the kitchen floor. From the top of his cage Harry squawked and anxiously flapped his wings. Peanuts came in to investigate, trying to catch the lobsters as if they were mice, only to find out that lobsters fight back.

Dad got out the tall boiler pot and began boiling water. We would have a great feast that night.

27

The people of Portobelo call themselves *Congos* and have a different culture from other Panamanians—even other black Panamanians. Descendants of African slaves brought in by Spaniards during the Spanish Empire, *Congos* are a proud mixture of tradition, mystery, and superstition from Africa, Spain, Catholicism, and Voodoo.

The last weekend before Grandma left for the States, our family went to the Atlantic Side to walk through Portobelo. This name, meaning, "beautiful port," was given by Christopher Columbus himself. Caught in a terrible storm on his fourth journey to the New World, he had discovered the U-shaped cove and quickly realized the inlet's potential.

In time, Portobelo became the most important city in the entire Spanish Empire. Gold, silver, and other treasures taken from mines and ruins of Peru were shipped along the Pacific Coast and unloaded at Panama City. From there the loot was loaded onto mules and the backs of slaves who trudged the heavy burdens to the port of *Nombre de Dios* on the Atlantic Side. There the fortune was loaded onto ships headed to Spain until, with the discovery of Portobelo inlet's much finer natural protection, the Spanish relocated the head of their operations.

Portobelo is home to three different forts: Fort Santiago and Fort Jeronimo on the mainland and Fort San Fernando across the bay on Drake Island. The body of the famous pirate, Sir Francis Drake, was enclosed in a lead coffin and sunk in this sun-kissed bay.

"We're not taking a boat across the bay," Dad announced before Debi and I could even get out of the van. We'd parked beside the largest fort, Fort Jeronimo. "You girls can find plenty to do right here."

Mom's look told Debi and me not to pester Dad, hoping he'd give in. We'd have to be content to stay on the mainland. We headed over to the royal customhouse, *Real Aduana*, a massive two-story concrete building next to the entrance of the old fort. Here bars of gold and silver had been counted and stacked like firewood before Spanish galleons shipped the treasure to Spain. On the covered porch, African slaves were bought and sold to transport goods across the isthmus and to load and unload ships during the Spanish regime.

An Italian had laid out the city of Portobelo, using a particular coral stone that withstood cannon fire. Dad had learned that not only did the stone resist cannon fire, even more curiously, cannon fire reinforced and strengthened it. That explained why so many of the structures were still standing. They couldn't be destroyed by cannon fire or any weapons. Even the jungle couldn't destroy the coral stone. All the jungle could do was to cover things up with vines and grasses.

While Grandma and the others took their time exploring the King's Customhouse, Debi and I grew restless.

"Let's go over to see the Black Christ," she suggested.

Mom approved. "Go ahead, girls."

So we headed over to the Church of San Felipe. The large white church off to the side of the main square still held regular services for the people of Portobelo. Like almost all churches in Panama, the door was unlocked and people were welcome to go in any time of the day or night.

A few dark-skinned *Congo* women were kneeling in a corner pew. Various statues of Jesus, Mary, and the apostles adorned the church's side walls, along with intricate wood-carvings of the Last Supper and the Crucifixion. At the front of the nave was an ornate altar with a life-sized statue of a man carrying a cross to the left—the Black Christ. A scarlet robe trimmed with gold fringe draped its shoulders. The statue had been carved from cocobolo wood, a very rare tropical rosewood. This naturally dark wood had blackened both from age and from the smoke of the candles kept continuously lit in front of it, until hundreds of years after its creation, the sculpture was extremely dark.

As we stood there gazing at it, Debi said, "Do you think Christ could really be black?"

"I don't know. Doesn't really seem to fit."

"Why not? What makes you think Christ is white?"

"I'm not sure what color Christ is. Think it matters?"

Debi shrugged. "Who knows?" She turned and read the English-language information cards posted on a stand, while I studied the Spanish version, picking out words I recognized. Debi wasn't the least bit impressed.

Several legends exist to explain how the Black Christ came to be in Portobelo. One story is that in the 16th century a ship was carrying the Black Christ to Colombia and stopped at the port for supplies. Five separate times this ship attempted to leave port, but each time a storm came up to prevent it. Finally, still caught in the cove by the fifth storm, the ship's captain threw the statue overboard to make the ship lighter. The storm abated and the ship could go on its way. It was said to have been fishermen who found the abandoned figure and brought it to the church.

Another explanation maintains that the statue was supposed to go to Taboga Island off Panama, but the Spanish shipper labeled the crate incorrectly so that the statue arrived in Portobelo instead. Attempts were made to send the statue on to Taboga, but once again, every time the ship was to leave the port, something happened to prevent it. In this legend like the other, the Christ figure was thrown overboard and washed up on shore.

Supposedly though, cocobolo wood does not float, so in either case the sculpted image should have sunk in the bay. However the statue came to be here, the people believed that it had magical powers and was destined to stay in Portobelo. It was given a place of honor in the little church and credited with many miracles.

The most notable instance was in a cholera epidemic in 1821, when the people prayed to the statue and their village was spared, while many cities on Panama's coast were devastated. Since then, without fail, October 21 marks the celebration of *El Cristo Negro*. In some years, as many as 60,000 believers make a pilgrimage to pay homage to the statue, including criminals seeking forgiveness for their crimes. During the celebration, at exactly eight P.M., eighty ablebodied men carry the statue from the church for a fourhour procession around the community. Then precisely at midnight, the statue is returned to its place beside the altar.

Twice a year the statue's robes are changed: a wine-red robe for the Black Christ festival and a purple one for Holy Week. Each robe is used only once and each one is donated by a worshiper. Some are simple, while others are quite ornately trimmed with gold.

By the church's side door, Debi and I saw a display of several previously worn robes with myriad bits of faded paper pinned to them. The paper scraps held supplicants' afflictions, pictures of wayward lovers or rebellious children, lottery tickets, and even the names of race horses, in the hope of a miracle from the Black Christ.

When we walked out of the church, we had to shade our eyes from the dazzling sunlight. While I paid no attention to an old woman selling handmade things at the side of the unpaved road, Debi was fascinated by the white-faced Capuchin monkey leashed to the woman's rusted folding chair. For a minute, the woman showed off her monkey, until she realized neither Debi nor I had any intention of buying a woven basket or a carved wooden cross. She tugged at the leash and the monkey climbed onto her lap, as she shooed us away with her hand. We were wasting her time.

Scattered over the remote hillsides on both the mainland and on Drake Island were smaller forts called *casamatas*. Here the Spanish had stored their gunpowder and arms. I pointed to one of the most distant and largest *casamatas*.

"Let's go to that one up there," I said, so Debi and I started up the hill.

"Judy," Mom called, seeing us cross the street, "take Connie with you." They were headed to the same church we had just left.

"Aww, c'mon," I moaned.

Taking Connie meant we couldn't go up as high. With no real path and the grass long and wet, climbing the hill would be quite an effort for Connie, whose stubby legs wouldn't make it all the way up. We'd have to go a closer, much smaller *casamata*.

I took Connie's hand, but Debi ran ahead. Before we'd even made it halfway, Connie complained she was tired. I pulled on her arm, almost dragging her along. "We're almost there. I don't know why you couldn't stay with Margie." I hoped she wouldn't sit in the long wet grass when she stopped to rest. "Do you want a piggyback ride?" I asked, before she had a chance to pout. I stooped down and let her climb on my back, figuring maybe I could catch up with Debi.

I was out of breath by the time we reached the *casamata* ruin, only to find it empty. Not that we had really expected to find anything, but we were still disappointed. The walls inside were black and the circular stones that led up to the watchtower crumbling. We climbed the stones anyway to get to the watchtower.

From that viewpoint, the horizon stretched for miles. Sailboats looked like little dots far out at sea. Debi searched hard, hoping to see shark fins poking out of the water. She swore that she saw at least two, but I claimed it was only the glare of the sun playing tricks on her eyes. She was not convinced. Bored, we came back down and returned to the main fort.

On our way down the hill, the pungent sweet jungle smells of rotting bananas and foliage at our backs were almost overpowering. We kept heading toward the ocean, welcoming the contrast of the faint salty breeze. We rejoined the rest of our family in the massive courtyard of Fort Jeronimo, where we climbed and straddled the heavy iron cannons facing the bay.

As we all looked out at the sea Dad told us the story of the English Admiral, Edward Vernon, who had captured Portobelo from the Spanish. His partner in this venture, the man who was with him at the capture, was George Washington's brother, Lawrence. Later, Lawrence had the estate where George Washington would eventually live named, "Mount Vernon," in honor of his stalwart admiral friend.

Both our parents were born and had spent much of their childhood in Washington, D.C. and Dad's father had done freelance work painting signs at Mount Vernon. Often Dad and his brother would wander through the estate after the tourists had gone home, waiting for their father to paint pinstripes on the image of George Washington's carriage emblazoned on official signs. It struck me that there we were, thousands of miles of away, in a relatively secluded and unknown part of the world, yet we were in touch with a part of our own American family history stretching back to a time long before the Panama Canal was even thought about.

"Isn't that something?" Grandma said. "Isn't that something?"

28

I was ten years old, and we had lived in the Canal Zone for almost five years. I had grown accustomed to the stark contrast between the unruly jungle and manmade barriers of concrete and steel. Life patterns in the Canal Zone were planned, organized, and structured, while the jungle promised chaos, confusion, spontaneity. The paradox was part of the charm of living in this exotic tropical home. Most days were hot, humid … and infinite.

Nondescript aimless sunny days merged into other nondescript aimless sunny days, when nothing seemed to happen. It was on just such a day that I walked down our road to the nicely landscaped circle that marked the end of Williamson Place. With no friends outside, I continued my walk past Clay Cliff and around the chain-link fence and "No Trespassing" sign—permanent reminders of yet another aimless sunny day.

My walk led me on past the lighthouse and toward the bridge. With no destination in mind, I kept going and stepped onto the bridge, knowing full well that once I crossed the bridge, I'd have to turn around and walk back. There was nothing for me on the other side, no buildings, no stores, no anything. The only thing on the other side of the bridge was the long solitary road that led to the town of Balboa, miles away.

At about the halfway point on the bridge, I stopped to gaze at the Chagres River stretching out in front of me. Barely a current moved. No boats were visible. Nobody was waterskiing or swimming from the banks of the few manmade islands.

Such an uneventful, laid-back kind of day would make anyone feel lazy, longing for a hammock. Though I hadn't completed my walk across the bridge, I turned around and began to walk back home, wondering what I would do next with the time stretching before me.

But then an irregular, thick tree branch down in the water caught my eye. It seemed to be floating in some current I hadn't noticed, a little way from the grassy river bank. I had often gone down to that grassy spot to soak my bare feet, hardened as they were from hot sidewalks along the roads. Captivated by this odd log that drifted in the stillness, yet not fully blending in with its surroundings, I stopped to focus on it. The longer I gazed, the realization finally dawned on me that it wasn't a log at all. It had eyes, which were staring right back at me.

The *Rio Chagres* is home to caimans, crocodiles, and American alligators. Although I'd been told the difference and had seen the different species at Summit Gardens, I couldn't tell which this one was. I did know that caimans are smaller, with a bony ridge between the eyes, while American alligators have a wider and shorter head, with a slightly different snout. As for the crocodile, it has a tooth that sticks out of its mouth even when its mouth is closed.

In spite of all that technical knowledge, at that moment, the species of the *Crocodylidae* mattered little to me. I knew they were all dangerous. When those big black eyes zeroed eerily in on me, I felt its penetrating stare, evil and menacing. Then the scaly-skinned body turned toward the bridge where I stood, unnerving me. I stiffened. My stomach knotted.

I reassured myself, *That creature couldn't possibly hurt you from way down there, Judy,* yet fear gripped me. Intellect and instinct clashed. Run or freeze in place?

I wrapped my arms around the steel handrail and held on to it firmly. From nowhere, a vision emerged of my feet somehow slipping so that I fell through the bars. *That's ridiculous*, I told myself.

I had walked this bridge many times without tripping, slipping, or even stubbing my toe, yet the gnawing feeling that my feet somehow would slip persisted. Closer and closer to the bridge, the dangerous animal floated as fear rooted me to the spot.

Did this menace think he could get me way up here on the bridge? Did he think I was fool enough to jump in and join him for a swim? Was he trying to hypnotize me to come to him? His deep sinister eyes taunted me to make the first move. I felt the connection between us—magnetic and intense. I dared not breathe nor blink. I don't know how long I stood there, mesmerized. Time stopped.

Then, from much too close, a long, slow, train whistle broke my trance. I would soon have to share this wooden bridge no more than a few feet from the heavy train speeding from Balboa. I knew from past experience how the bridge rattled and shook when that powerful engine ran across it. Ordinarily I loved the thrilling encounter of being close to the forceful rush of its steel energy, but not today. I was terrified that any movement on the bridge might cause me to fall.

I released my hold on the rail and ran as hard and fast as I could to the end of the bridge and kept running down the sidewalk. I ignored the grassy path to the lighthouse and to my street beyond. Instead, I ran all the way to the red stairs. I wanted to keep my feet on cement. I wanted to be visible to people coming and going in their cars from Gamboa. I wanted to be seen!

The order and routine of civilization settled my nerves, as I saw the Canal Zone from that moment on in a way I hadn't before. On one hand, I felt a deep sense of protection and security in its pristine-manicured grounds. On the other hand, I knew without a doubt that we were in the jungle, which had its own ways, ways which were not always forgiving.

I knew of kids who had jumped off the Gamboa Bridge into the river below, a daring act that lots of Gamboa kids did with complete abandon. I had always thought that one day I would join them, but suddenly I decided not be one of those kids. The challenge no longer appealed to me.

The Gamboa Bridge

Balboa
1971–1977

Our house in Balboa

29

When I was eleven, we left Gamboa. Dad's job had been transferred to the electronic shop based out of Balboa and Canal Zone policy mandated that employees had to reside in the town where they worked.

For seven years, we'd lived in our house in the small town of Gamboa. Most of the kids in my class had started school with me, in the back corner room of the Gamboa gym. We'd gone to each others' birthday parties, joined each others' Vacation Bible School programs regardless of personal church affiliation, and knew who'd seen snow and who hadn't. We recognized each other's hand-me-down clothes from our older brothers and sisters who had worn them the year before. We knew whose side to be on for rotten-mango fights and where the best skim-boarding ponds would be during rainy season.

Each year, I could write classmates' names on my Valentine cards without even looking at the class list. I could tell you that David loved science, Roger loved music, Cindy loved horses, and Bobby loved Laurie. Mrs. Norris had already promised that next month I'd be the captain of the safety patrols, but now I'd be gone. I'd waited a long time for my turn as Patrol Leader, but I wouldn't even be a patroler in my new school.

The previous year, my family had gone through several other changes. As Cocoa grew older, he didn't tolerate family life the way he used to, so, we took him to a wildlife preserve, where the trader told us a Japanese zoo had requested an adult coatimundi. Cocoa would be shipped to Japan. Margie sold her horse and Harry went to live with Grandma in Florida, where we would see him in the summers.

Maria was gone as well. The trouble began when Mom found out that Debi and I were telling Maria to clean our room and do our chores. That made Mom angry and when she heard Debi and me both demand that Maria bring us each a glass of water while we sat on the couch reading comic books, Mom said we'd crossed a line. She wasn't about to have her girls thinking they were entitled princesses. Her daughters would be independent young ladies, who did for themselves. Despite all of our pleading, Mom's mind was set. Maria had to go.

My life had long been a comfortable routine. I liked where I lived and had no desire to move. Nevertheless, our lives were changing and reluctantly, I had to change, too.

Balboa, the administrative center of the Canal Zone, was about a mile between Sosa Hill and Ancon Hill. On the other side of Sosa Hill was the Canal, while on the other side of Ancon Hill was Panama City. The Panama Canal Administration Building sat like a sentry, high on grassy Ancon Hill, its windows providing a bird's-eye view of the town proper and the comings and goings of the workers and their dependents. Balboa's narrow roads, like those of all Canal Zone towns, were smoothly paved, the landscapes meticulously manicured and a feeling of order dominated the senses.

The center of Balboa covered perhaps two city blocks and included the nondescript company commissary, the only company shoe store, a company hardware and furniture store, and a post office. There were two private banks, a credit union, the Jewish Welfare Board, several Christian churches, and a few civic clubs, such as the Elks and Knights of Columbus.

The town also boasted the Balboa Bowling Alley, a skating rink, and the only high school on the Pacific Side. Like all the other towns, it had the requisite movie theater and a large swimming pool. Of all the townships, Balboa was the busiest and, if you included such housing areas as Diablo and Los Rios, had a population of not quite seven thousand Americans.

"We'll be city folk," Debi said, sucking in her cheeks and using her best Grandma-voice impression.

On Sunday after church following Dad's announcement, we began looking for a new place to live. First we drove over to the housing office next to the train station, where a list of available housing was posted on the bulletin board. We sat in the car, while Mom and Dad looked at the list and Mom wrote down addresses of vacant or soon-to-be vacant houses with at least three bedrooms. Then we drove through the various neighborhoods to consider the houses, before Dad placed a bid.

Houses were assigned based on seniority and since Dad had just seven years of service, our choices were limited. Dad could be competing with people who had eighteen or more service years and were upgrading to nicer homes. Timing and luck were essential to claim a good house. With time running out, we found nothing suitable.

Then one day after work, Dad came home early with a set of keys from the housing office. He'd won a bid on one of the houses we'd driven by. "Let's go look at this place," he said. "This could be it."

We drove back to Balboa and veered up the hill past the Union Church. The houses that lined two-laned Tavernilla Street were old tropical quarters that housed four families—two separate residences on the bottom floor, two on the top. Our prospective home was on the second floor.

Although Debi and I were thrilled that three other families lived in the same building, Mom was not. Not only would we have families living in our same building, but similar four-family homes lined Tavernilla Street. It seemed like more families lived on this one street than lived in all of Gamboa!

The sidewalk and road were alive with kids riding their bikes, jumping rope, and playing marbles. Debi and I knew we'd have friends just by walking out the door. The faded wooden four-plex sat on a hill, and from the front door we could see the grassy Prado leading to the elementary school and the Admin Building on Ancon Hill. We'd be close enough to walk or ride our bikes to the clubhouse, pool, and church.

"Of course, climbing back up the hill might be a little bit exhausting," Debi observed, "but we'd get used to it." For the most part, the location was ideal.

We all walked up the stairs to the vacant residence and Dad opened the door … onto a long narrow hallway rather like a lane in a bowling alley. Debi and I read each other's thoughts. This would be fun! I pictured the two of us setting up bottles and rolling a ball down the hallway. I imagined having friends over for bowling parties. Excitedly, Debi and I started to plan where we'd set up each bowling pin, as Connie and Margie followed Mom and Dad to see the rest of the place.

Doors from the hallway opened into the various bedrooms and the kitchen. This apartment-style home was much smaller than our Gamboa house. The wooden floor lacked a proper shine, and the exposed 2x4s weren't smooth. Dutifully, Mom checked out each room, disappointment showing clearly on her face. Although she loved people, she also enjoyed privacy and space—this place had neither. We climbed back into the car and headed home. Dad returned the key the next day. Maybe we'd find something else.

A week later Dad came home with another key. This

time we checked out a house in Los Rios. As usual, the housing area had an elementary school and a community pool. The houses there were newer, more modern cement-block buildings and they didn't sit high on cement stilts that would require us to climb stairs to enter. The drawback to that was no open space underneath the house for extra storage and entertaining. Yet many Zonians preferred these houses, which they nicknamed "chicken coops."

Again, Mom checked each room. This place was a duplex, much like our home in Gamboa, but our duplex in Gamboa was spacious and open, while this one was small and cramped. Gamboa had grass, plants, trees, even jungle between the houses, with a clear view of the Panama Canal that paralleled the main Gamboa Road.

Here in Los Rios, there were houses, cement, and more houses. Oh, sure, there were the familiar cookie-cutter immaculate green yards metered out to each residence and a little clump of jungle along one far edge, but, for the most part, there was far more concrete than shrubbery, far more white than green. No wonder it was called a chicken coop.

Even though two of Mom's best friends lived in houses of the chicken-coop variety and each of them had four children, Mom didn't think this was the house for us.

"Let's wait one more week," she said, walking back to the car. "Maybe something else will come available." Dad would try and get us another week or two before we had to decide. There was a deadline.

A few days later, as we tried to resign ourselves to living in smaller quarters with more neighbors crammed all around us than we'd know what to do with, Dad came home more excited than I'd seen him in a while. We had a new home and he wanted to take us to it right then.

Margie had to raise a question, "We're not even going to have a say in this?"

Mom had proudly taught us to voice our opinions, usually rendering Dad helpless. Not this time. He stood his ground and hurried us along. In the car, Dad's face lit up as he told Mom that he'd learned about a newly remodeled house. There wasn't time for the family to do our customary drive-by before the bidding, so on a whim, he had put in for the residence.

It happened that Louie, one of the guys who worked in the same company division as Dad, had put in a bid for the same house. When Dad realized that, he lost hope that his bid would win, because Louie had many more years of service. Even so, Dad had come in second on the list for the house. That was a good surprise. An even better one came when Louie turned down the house and Dad won the bid.

"Unbelievable!" he told us. "Simply unbelievable! A man with seven years in the company doesn't get quarters like this."

We drove straight through downtown Balboa and turned right at the YMCA. The road forked at Empire Street, going into La Boca area, but we continued down Amador Road. Only one side of the street had houses. The other side was a grassy hill that formed one boundary of the La Boca housing area. We turned left a few feet before the only gate to Fort Amador, a Navy/Marine base that also housed a Smithsonian Research Center, the Causeway, and Scout Island.

And there, on a hidden side street called Bougainvillea, stood our new house. I stepped out into the hot, sticky afternoon to see. A single-family, French-style building with large eaves to block direct sunlight from glass jalousie windows, this wooden house, like our home in Gamboa, was raised on cement pilings. Zonians had fondly nicknamed this style of structure "birdhouses."

The house was on a corner, surrounded by a living fence

of tight hedges offering a private screen for the grassy yard. Only a few feet from the back stairs were flourishing banana, lime, and lemon trees, and various palms, hibiscus, and bougainvillea created a mini-tropical retreat.

A road and tall chain-link fence marked the boundaries of Fort Amador. Across the street, another "birdhouse" residence bordered the Bay of Panama. This quiet, secluded side street lined with eight similar single-family homes made Bougainvillea Avenue a desirable neighborhood. Nestled at the far end of the block was a community playground closed off by an industrial chain-link fence. Just a few feet beyond was a cliff and the spacious blue cove. Across the water, we could see Panama City's ragged skyline.

Tucked away from the busyness of Balboa, this house was barely a mile apart from the activity. A stop for public buses a few feet from the back corner of the house would be my link to the Canal Zone world and the school bus stop was only two houses down. Yet if I had to, I could walk the mile or so to Balboa Elementary.

As we explored the house, I watched Mom's face for her reaction. No long bowling alley, no irregular angles. The living room was spacious and rectangular, with room enough to section off a formal dining area. A swinging door in one corner led to the kitchen. A long narrow hallway connected the four bedrooms, and off the master bedroom was a small second bathroom. Two bathrooms! The six of us had shared one bathroom for so long, a second bathroom would be a dream!

After her walkthrough Mom came back to the living room with a nod and big smile. "This is it," she pronounced.

We left rejoicing in our new soon-to-be home. We were going to be Balboa city folks.

30

I dreaded being the new kid introduced to a class of strangers. I imagined myself looking around the classroom hoping to find a friendly face, wondering which desk was assigned to me. The other students would probably watch me, curious. I'd seen that happen to other kids. New kids fresh from the States easily made friends, because they had so much to talk about. But I was from Gamboa, which didn't qualify me as new.

On my last day at Gamboa Elementary, my class surprised me with a farewell party featuring cupcakes and other treats. Mr. Miskowsky had each of my classmates say something nice about me. I felt embarrassed, but I also felt good. I knew I'd see most of them the next year in Curundu Junior High, plus I could take the bus and visit them as often as I wanted, and they could visit me in Balboa. Still, it would be different. Knowing I would miss my Gamboa life, I wondered how long it would take before the new life felt normal.

Unfortunately, the company's packers and movers came on one of Panama's rainiest days in years. Life in Panama was always the same, until it wasn't. This wasn't the typical dense two-hour storm, with the sun returning and soaking the water back into the clouds, creating humidity so thick you could slice it with your hand. No, this day had a different kind of rain.

It began early in the morning and didn't stop until late that night. It rained so much the roads flooded, cars stalled in newly formed pockets of water, and our belongings were soaked.

Undeterred, the workers packed, moved, and set us up in our new home in less than a day. We'd have to live out of damp boxes for a few days until Mom found new places for everything.

In this house, our kitchen, bedrooms and hall bathroom were connected by an inner hallway that framed the living room and dining area. We could actually walk to each bedroom, the bathroom, kitchen and outside door without being seen by anyone in the living room. This meant that when our parents had visitors, I could come in from outside, go to the kitchen or the bedroom, and leave again without being noticed. It also meant that when Mom hollered for someone to do a chore, I could go in the opposite direction and slip out of the house without her seeing me.

No longer would I have to share a bedroom with Debi. I had my own room, next to the kitchen. Margie had her own room, too, at the front of the house. It had two doors, one to the living room and the other to the bedroom that Debi and Connie shared. My parents' room was across the hall.

Dad said Margie and I could paint our bedroom walls any color we wanted, as long as we did the painting. Margie chose navy blue and dark green, and Dad helped her put up a black light to shine on her posters. Instead of painting my room, I settled for posting my pinups of Donnie Osmond and David Cassidy ripped from the pages of *Teen Star* to my walls.

"You know that looks tacky," Margie said when she saw my room. Her use of the word, "tacky," struck me funny, as I'd actually used thumbtacks to put up my pictures. When I tried to explain why I thought it was funny, she just rolled her eyes, giving me the 'Will You Grow Up Look.'

And that wasn't all she had to say. "Why do you cram your books in the bookcase like that? It would look much nicer if you arranged them in a neat organized way."

I stared at my bookcase, trying to figure out what she meant. Did she mean I should put all the Nancy Drew books together on one shelf and all the Happy Hollister books together on another? Or did she mean to put my favorite books on one side and my not-so-favorite books on another? Maybe she meant I should put books of one size on one shelf, smaller books on the other. Or I could put the books I planned to keep on a top shelf, and books I planned to trade on a bottom one. What about comic books? Should they go on the same shelf as the hardbacks? Trying to organize called for too many decisions. I decided not to decide—it was simpler.

I thought I'd have a look at Margie's room, so in I went. Her windows were open to let out the paint fumes and her big posters were lined up as if she'd used a yardstick to make them even. Her record albums were lined up vertically in the bookcase and it wouldn't have surprised me to find them alphabetized. Her bed was made, the spread neatly covering matching sheets and pillowcases. Though I never had the patience to find matching sheets and pillowcases in the linen closet, I had to admit it would have made my bed look nice. Eye-catching pillows in various sizes, shapes, and colors propped against the wall and invited a person to lean back and snuggle in with a book.

A throw rug in front her bed boasted a peace sign—a rug Dad hated. To him, the peace sign was a sacrilegious parody—an upside-down cross. When he said it showed disrespect for the Crucifixion, Margie asked him where he got his crazy ideas. She was allowed to keep the rug, but Dad wanted her to know its true meaning. Dad also wanted her to know he didn't like it.

Long hanging strands of tiny plastic beads hid the closed door that separated Margie's bedroom from Debi's and Connie's. In front of this door was a smaller throw rug featuring a whimsical green frog on a lily pad and thick black letters announcing "My Pad"—as if we needed reminding that this space was hers.

Beside the little rug, atop a small round table was a stack of flimsy boxes with Chinese lettering, each one for a separate fragrance of incense and in front of these boxes, smoke curled upward from a carved wooden incense burner. The scent of vanilla hadn't yet overcome the paint fumes and the humid air from opened windows.

Margie had been watching me. "What do you think?"

"It's perfect."

I meant it—I thought it was absolutely perfect. She had taken a small, ordinary, dreary space and made a warm inviting room. This was a place where friends could come and hang out. They would talk for hours and listen to music while the black light strobed trendy posters. They would share secrets and dreams while planning their lives and figuring out what to do next weekend. They would do what friends did, including blocking out pesky younger sisters who didn't know how to be cool.

"Just remember," Margie warned as I was leaving, "this is my room. You stay out of mine and I will stay out of yours."

She didn't have to tell me that—I knew it.

Debi and Connie had the largest bedroom of all. The same two white twin beds that were in the Gamboa room I had shared with Debi were now arranged by the room's only window. A matching white dresser with a generous mirror faced the beds from the opposite wall. My sisters would have plenty of room to play, once the moving boxes were finally emptied and belongings put in new places. Mom promised to paint and decorate the walls once we were settled. Meanwhile, it was a species of ordered chaos.

It felt odd not to be sharing a room with Debi. We'd shared a room for so long that it seemed almost unnatural to be by myself. Debi promised she'd come to spend the night in my room, as long as it wasn't a school night.

Everyone loved having all the rooms on one floor. No more climbing stairs to put school books away, to go to bed, or even to use the bathroom. The only stairs we had to climb now were the outside stairs that led into the house.

Beneath the house we had a more private and finished space than the underneath of our Gamboa house. Here, an enclosed garage divided the underneath in half. One half was already partitioned off for entertainment space. Dad brought in a huge, heavy, wooden picnic table that would comfortably seat twelve people on a side, and over at the edge of the space he hung our wooden swing from the joists of the floor above.

On the other side of the garage Dad set up a full-sized ping-pong table, and in the tiny side yard, a tetherball pole. Impenetrable shrubbery fenced our little side yard from our neighbor's matching house.

The backyard measuring twenty-five feet or so wasn't as large as our previous backyard, so our swing set looked out of place crammed in amid the foliage. The fruit trees overshadowed most of the grassy space, but the small yard didn't matter, for right down the street was a spacious playground. Why be alone in a small yard when there was always a gaggle of kids swinging, playing kick-the-can or marbles, or sitting around talking at the playground until the streetlights came on? It was almost impossible to live in the Canal Zone and not make friends.

Our new house seemed just right. Still, at night when I lay in bed in my private room, my windows no longer vibrated from passing ships and I no longer saw the beam of light gliding across the wall. Instead of listening to Debi's incessant chatter before I fell asleep, all I heard now was the hum of my window air conditioner and the hoarse croak of serenading tree frogs, like a soothing heartbeat.

31

Debi and I were both nervous and excited the first day we rode the school bus to Balboa Elementary. Margie's bus to Curundu Junior High had left earlier that morning and Connie wasn't old enough for school. To celebrate the occasion, Debi and I both wore our best dresses and nicest shorts underneath. We shared a bus seat.

Much larger and more impressive than the wooden school building in Gamboa, our new school was a solid concrete structure with stately arches gracing a porch entrance. Directly in front of its main doors was the Goethals Monument, a memorial to George Washington Goethals, the U.S. Army engineer who oversaw construction of the Panama Canal. The rectangle of white marble soared upward, reflecting the sunlight, with three protruding tiers about midway up to symbolize the three locks of the Canal.

The monument was also a fountain with an interior recycling pump to create a continuous flow of water from the top down over each tier before splashing to the bottom. Some people tossed coins into the shallow pool as if it were a wishing well, though Zonian kids cooled their feet in it. Occasionally a bored Zonian teen would pour soap powder into the water, so that as the pump recycled the water, a world of soap bubbles was the result.

On the other side of the monument, a large patch of trees and grass bordered a narrow two-lane road and the grounds of Balboa High School. From my school bus window, I watched high-school students casually smoking as

Gothels Monument in Balboa between Balboa High School and Balboa Elementary

they waited under a tree for the bell to ring and ROTC students practicing formations in a side yard. I imagined myself in high school, carrying my books, chatting with friends from Gamboa.

Mom had already registered Debi and me in the new school, and we had been assigned classrooms. Balboa Elementary had three stories, with classrooms on each floor, its inner walls framing an open courtyard. A large tree grew right up in the center of the school. During the rainy season, rain poured into the courtyard, hammered quite loudly against the school's roof, and beat against the windowpanes—a considerable volume of sound.

My sixth-grade class was one of four on the third floor, while Debi's fourth-grade room was on the second floor. When the time came for school to begin, we went in and walked to our respective floors. From the inner balcony where the line of sixth graders waited for our teacher to open our door, I could see Debi waiting on the second floor. All excited, I waved and she waved back.

Since my first day of kindergarten, I'd never been in a class of more than seventeen students. Now I was one of twenty-five. Not all lived in the Canal Zone or were Americans. Some were Panamanians, whose parents paid tuition to get their children a U.S. education. Parents or private drivers brought these classmates from Panama City.

After my teacher assigned me a desk, I immediately wondered which reading group I'd be in, hoping desperately that in a class that big, I wouldn't have to read in front of everyone. Not enough time, surely. Not that I couldn't read. I could read quite well, but I preferred to read silently, rather than in front of people. And this seemed like a *lot* of people.

My teacher, Mrs. Stephenson, told me she was new, too. This was her first year teaching in Balboa. Her husband was in the Air Force and she'd only been in the Canal Zone a few months. Right away, she gave me a reading part in the spring concert coming up the next month—two lines during the sixth-grade presentation of the "Emperor's New Clothes." We'd be performing for parents and guests in the courtyard. She didn't give me a chance to tell her that speaking in front of people was something I'd rather not do and she seemed so happy to have given me the two lines, I reluctantly agreed.

I met Debi at noon. We could no longer go home for lunch. Instead, we'd be part of the group that stayed at school and carried a bag lunch. We sat at one of the long tables in a back corner of the gym. Debi made friends easily. We finished our sandwiches quickly and went outside to stand in line to play tetherball.

The girl in front of me said, "Are you any good?" I nodded, because I thought I was pretty good at it.

"You'll have to be," she said. "Dyra is playing."

I looked up to the front of the line where two players faced each other on the tetherball court just like the one at Gamboa Elementary. There was a small circle with a tall pole in the middle and a long thin rope hanging from the pole attached to a yellow ball. A white-painted line divided the circle in half. My favorite side of the court was always the left side, the winner side. My game plan was always the same: Start in the right side of the circle, beat the previous winner, move over to the left side and face a new challenger.

In the left side was Dyra, a tall, strong-looking girl from my new sixth-grade class. My assigned seat was only three desks away from hers, and she had smiled at me when I sat down. Now, I learned that she'd been the reigning champion of Balboa Elementary tetherball for several years and many kids were eager for her to move on to Curundu Junior High. One by one, a challenger stepped into the circle and one by one, lost. The line moved pretty fast, too.

Sometimes when I'd played tetherball before, a game had lasted five or ten minutes, with the ball flying from player to player. But the rounds with Dyra weren't lasting nearly that long.

Finally it was my turn. I stepped into the right side of the circle and, being the challenger, served first. I punched the ball high and hard, a serve that had always worked for me.

Dyra's fist met the ball without hesitation in a solid thud that wrapped that rope so thoroughly around the pole I never had a chance to jump up and block it. In one quick move, I was out.

Debi was next, repeating my performance. It seemed pointless to get back in the tetherball line and face tough Dyra again. Maybe we'd have better luck at Four-Square. If not, tomorrow I'd bring my marbles. I had brought two good steelies from Gamboa, so I knew I could beat someone with those.

Debi's new friend, Lori, motioned us to follow her. We hurried into the tree line next to the play yard and crept a few feet into the bush, where a drainage ditch flowed into the underground tunnels that led to the Canal. Some other kids were gnawing on sugar cane. A boy from Debi's class, Robbie, uncovered a sharp kitchen knife from under the leaves, carved off a piece of sugar-cane stalk, stripped the outer bark, and handed us both a small segment, so we sat under a tree and licked the juice from our sugar cane until lunchtime was over. I began to think living in Balboa would suit me just fine.

32

K im and her family lived seven houses from us. I could be at their house in under four minutes or less, if I cut through two backyards. Kim was almost a year younger and in fifth grade, but that didn't matter. We became friends and she showed me life in Balboa.

This port town on the Pacific Side was considerably larger than Gamboa. I could still walk or ride my bike everywhere I wanted to go, but it took me longer to get from one place to another. Balboa was spread out, with lots of little hidden areas.

The jungly bush that always threatened to overtake Gamboa was controlled here in Balboa. All the houses and other buildings seemed more noticeable, set in the precisely manicured Canal Zone landscaping. We no longer lived on the Canal's bank and I missed watching ships transit. In less than five minutes though, I could ride my bike to the Balboa Yacht Club and watch the ships pass by there. This I often did.

Most military bases and townships in the Canal Zone had a movie theater. The one in Balboa was worlds apart from the other theaters, especially Gamboa's. The Balboa Movie Theater was modern, concrete and, most important, air-conditioned. Dad and I agreed that it was one of the few pretty buildings in the Canal Zone. I loved going to movies at the Balboa Theater, a more upscale experience than the ones we went to in Gamboa. On Friday and Saturday nights, all the theaters ran two movies: a more family-oriented early show, and a late show more suitable for adults. Some theaters offered a Friday-night extra—an Owl Show that let out after midnight. Usually it was a horror movie.

After the Owl Show, we'd have to leave by the side doors to find ourselves walking the abandoned streets of Balboa. At that time of night, the commissary, clubhouse, bowling alley, and other buildings were locked up and dark. No buses ran and there were hardly any cars on the streets. The streetlights made flickering shadows so that even the familiar looked creepy. Sometimes either Kim's or my parents picked us up after a movie, but at other times we walked home in the dark eerie quiet.

Here, unlike the Gamboa Movie Theater, I didn't have to stand outside to purchase a ticket, then walk upstairs to the screening room. The Balboa Theater had a fancy outer lobby with posters of coming attractions and a rope of gold braid indicating the ticket line. Once Kim and I bought our tickets there, we walked through the heavy wooden doors into the inner lobby. The right side of that lobby was the ladies' side, its walls papered with a creamy pastel design of interlocking swirls. An oversized mirror hung on one wall, with framed pictures on the two other walls. Several elaborately cushioned chairs were set in groups and the soft light of floor lamps made shadows on the red paisley carpet for a sense of welcome and grace. From the corner, a hallway led to an equally ornate ladies' restroom, by far the nicest I'd ever seen in a public building.

By stark contrast, the left side of the lobby was the men's side. It had fewer chairs, which were heavy and oversized. Only two floor lamps stood on that side of the lobby. Tall silver chalice ashtrays beside each chair held a few stubbed-out cigarette butts. No framed pictures livened up the serviceable brownish wallpaper and there, too, a hallway led from a corner to the men's restroom.

When I asked Dad why the men's side was so plain, he said it was because men didn't need pampering.

"Too bad," I said, glad I was a girl.

It was my habit to study the rows of candy on display in the glass-fronted concession stand that separated the two lobbies. My hope was that some of the candy we'd enjoyed in the States would appear in the Canal Zone. Usually, the rows displayed the same limited variety. Behind the counter, an industrial-sized popcorn popper spit out fluffy white kernels, which the concession worker scooped into red-and-white bags. Of course,. there was a soda fountain and a cash register. Like the lobby, the concession stand glistened and sparkled and I imagined I was in a New York City theater.

It was an altogether different story at the Quarry Heights military headquarters theater. An old wooden theater, that one sold hotdogs and beer and the restrooms were next to the movie screen. To use the restroom, you had to walk up steps onto the stage and when you opened the restroom door, light from inside flashed across the screen. Sometimes moviegoers shouted, "Shut the door!" I never used that restroom, no matter how desperately I needed to go.

No matter which theater I went to, the one thing I always wanted to buy was a chocolate bar. Before the lights went off for the movie, I'd unwrap it and break the bar into tiny pieces, scrutinizing each particle. Once satisfied that it was bug-free, I'd wrap the bits back up to enjoy during the movie.

The Balboa Theater, my favorite, had an inclined hallway that led from the center of the lobby to the seats and the stage with the gigantic screen. To enter the screening room, you had to pass between blackout curtains that were closed to cut off light and noise from the lobby once the movie started. If I didn't see a movie usher, I ran my hand down these thick velvety drapes.

A waist-high partition separated the screening room into two sections. The section nearest the stage sloped downward, putting the front row of seats a few feet in front of the stage. At each end of the stage was a set of steps to the platform, with heavy curtains at each side of the screen.

It was on this stage that I would watch magic shows and high-school band and chorus concerts. A couple of times during the Owl Show, I even saw a streaker. I cheered and booed with the rest of the audience at the shadowy naked figure.

The balcony had rows of seats leading up to the door of the projection room. There was also a small sound-proof room with more seats and a crib, called the "cry room," with a large plate-glass window facing the movie screen. That arrangement allowed mothers with babies to watch the movie without worrying that their babies' noise might disrupt the movie experience for everyone else. Sometimes I sneaked in to watch the movie from there just to see what it was like.

If the Balboa Theater had bats, I never saw one. Certainly none ever came flying over the screen and the tops of our heads. That theater was so opulent and ornate with carved architectural curves and scrolls on the walls, I don't think a bat would have dared to venture in. Nor were there any screened windows that would have let other creatures in, though sometimes an occasional small lizard did scurry across the floor. After all, we lived in a tropical area and only so much could be done to keep the jungle out.

Kim and I had no preference as to seats. If we went to the Owl Show, we sat closer to the screen, because the balcony was roped off. If we went to an early movie, we might sit in the balcony because younger kids sat in the lower section. If we saw a group of our friends, we sat by them or, if we saw a boy we liked, we sat close enough to be noticed. Other than that, we were fairly flexible about where we sat.

Kim and I didn't always spend our money going to the movies. Sometimes we spent it at Amador Beach, if we managed to get a ride. My family didn't join the members-only beach at the end of the Causeway, but Kim's family belonged. I often went there as her guest. We'd spend our day relaxing on towels spread on the sand, wave to friends cruising by on the Causeway and stuff ourselves with hot *empanadas* fresh from the Snack Shack.

When we were absolutely broke, which was often the case, we went to her house or mine—it didn't matter which. Kim and I played long games of Monopoly or Parcheesi. We relaxed on our beds and read comic books, talked about our lives, and listened to the radio. If it were late enough in the afternoon for SCN to be broadcasting, we watched TV.

Sometimes on school nights, I'd go over to her house after supper and work on homework at her kitchen table or just sit and talk. From her kitchen window, we could hear the loud monstrous tree toads. I often stayed at Kim's house until Mom or one of my sisters telephoned, reminding me that it was a school night and I should have been home long ago. I'd run through the backyards, trying not to step on or even see the hideous toads that loved the night. I hopped over any fallen palm fronds and hurried onto the sidewalk that led to my house. Then I would pick up the phone to make plans with Kim for the next day.

33

Debi and I joined the same Girl Scout troop as Kim and her younger sister. We couldn't believe our luck that we'd join this troop just in time for an upcoming overnight camping trip on the Atlantic Side. For our first time camping on this side, we'd be taking the train. Our Scout leaders had already made arrangements for the conductor to stop at a designated spot, where we would unload and hike almost a mile to the campsite. Dad promised to drop us off at the train station early.

Rainy season wasn't due to start for a couple of weeks, but this had been an odd year. We'd already had harder and earlier rains than usual, and on that morning when we got off the train, the hot damp air pressed into the pores of our skin, as if we were sweating inside our bodies. Not even the leaders had the energy to try to raise our morale. We were eager to set up camp and find relief from the bruising heat, for it was not a day to carry tents and backpacks.

Finally we reached our wooded campsite. The entrance to the Atlantic Side of the Canal was just a few yards away, though the dense trees blocked our view of the water. Kim and I shrugged off our backpacks and walked over to a sloppy pile of tents. Clearly, the last troop that had used the tents had not stored them properly, for canvas and rope were a tangled mess.

We struggled alongside the other Scouts to separate one tent from another, until we managed to break one away from the pile. However, in the damp, soggy soil, our tent stakes refused to take hold and stand straight. We just could not get those wooden spikes firmly into the ground.

As I pounded the last stake in, Kim sighed. "I guess our tent will just have to lean," she said, as we put our sleeping bags and backpacks inside.

"No matter," I said, surveying the other tents. "Everyone else's looks the same."

We laid out our bedrolls and organized our clothes, flashlights, and gear. Leaving the tent, we zipped both the inner and outer zippers of the mosquito netting to seal out scorpions, tarantulas, and other unwanted crawlers, though we tied open the outside flap to let air circulate, figuring humid air was better than no air at all.

One of the leaders and her husband had driven to the camp in a Jeep, which they parked at the edge of the clearing next to a solitary cement building that housed two bathrooms with a couple of toilets and sinks, but no showers. We were to use the two heavy-duty hoses, coiled on a slab, connected to outside faucets.

Kim and I went to help carry the paper sacks of groceries and supplies into the rudimentary kitchen, where two older Scouts were setting up heavy fans to circulate the warm air coming through the screened windows. The room was bare except for an industrial sink, two old white refrigerators and several long metal tables.

The rest of the afternoon went by quickly as we did crafts, prepared and cooked our tin-foil dinners on the campfire, put our plates and eating utensils into mesh bags and washed them by dunking them in the water that had boiled on another fire. I hung my dunking bag next to Kim's on a clothesline stretched between two trees so that our dishes would be dry and ready for breakfast.

Night falls quickly in the jungle. Before long, we were standing around a big campfire roasting marshmallows and giggling. But then, as if someone had flipped a switch, everyone got quiet. We'd all heard the sound at the same time, a peculiar chittering sound we didn't recognize. Then in one horrifying moment, the ground came alive with squarish red-and-black land crabs about the size of quarters. Thousands of tiny crabs seemed to emerge out of the dirt to swarm over every inch of the campground, crawling over everything in their path, sparing nothing.

All we girls, plus our Scout leaders, screamed and ran into the building, desperately trying not to step on the crabs or let any scamper over our feet. In a flash, we quickly climbed onto the tables to get out of the way as hordes of the crabs even invaded the floor of the building.

This was worse than any Owl Show! None of us had ever seen anything like it. Where on earth had the crabs come? They couldn't have been here when we put up our tents, because we would have seen them when we pounded in the stakes.

Then, just as suddenly as they had come, they were gone. In less than a minute, every last one disappeared, leaving no clue as to where they went.

Still standing on our table with Debi beside us, Kim and I exchanged a look of disbelief.

One brave leader got off her table with her flashlight and began to search for the crabs while the rest of us held our breath. Then another leader got down and once we realized the leaders were fine, we climbed hesitantly off the tables, too.

There was not one crab to be found, no evidence of a single crab. We found out later that the crab invasion is a natural phenomenon in parts of Panama at certain times of the year. We didn't know that then though and afterward, Kim and I lay in the darkness of our tent wondering if the crabs would come back. The choir of jungle noises also kept us from sleeping. What might happen next?

Just as I began to drift asleep, lightning flashed across

the side of the tent and thunder clashed. Wind howled through the tree limbs and shook our tent. The skies opened, and the rain poured down by the bucketful.

I scooted to the screen doorway of our tent to watch, squinting to make out the shadow of the building several feet away. The yellow light from the few burning light bulbs inside flickered through the wall of rain in the darkness. Then came a whoosh, and one tent was completely down.

Kim and I looked at each other. Our own tent was beginning to cave in the pounding rain. It wouldn't hold another five minutes. We scrambled to don our rain ponchos over our shorts, shoved our feet into muddy tennis shoes, and grabbed our flashlights. The tent flap beat wildly in the wind. We ran toward the building fighting the rain as it slapped our bodies and plastered our wet hair against our faces.

Some of the other girls were already there sitting at the tables, propping their tired heads up with their elbows. I sat next to Debi and Ann to watch the flashes of lightning through the screened windows. We placed bets on whose tent would go down next, cheered for the tents that still stood, groaned as other tents collapsed. Finally we laid our heads on our arms and fell asleep to wait for morning.

When day dawned, it was a miserable one. Small tree limbs and flattened tents littered the campground. The clothesline holding our mesh bags had snapped and coiled around a tree, with the bags holding our plates, cups, and flatware scattered helter-skelter in branches, underbrush, and mud.

Kim and I walked over to our crumpled tent to begin the cleanup in humidity so thick I could practically see water droplets in the air. We all spent the morning dragging our sodden tents to the cement slab and hosing off the mud, laying them out to dry as well as best we could.

Several hours later we rolled them up and piled them into the Jeep, then we propped our gear against the back of the building and waited for early afternoon to hike back to board the train for home.

From the train seat next to me, Debi pointed through the open window. "Judy, look over there. I think that's Dad."

A small-engine plane flew low parallel to the train. Sure enough, Dad!

As Debi and I waved wildly from the train window, Dad tipped his plane's wing and disappeared from view.

Debi looked across the corridor, to see Dad on the other side! We ran over to that side and again waved wildly out the other open window.

Our fellow Girl Scouts joined us, going from window to window, from one side of the train to the other as Dad maneuvered his plane back and forth over its roof.

"There he is!" someone shouted.

All of us ran to the windows, thrusting out our arms and waving.

"He's behind us!" someone else shouted.

We all giggled and shrieked with delight, running to the back seats and waving.

"To the front!" someone else hollered.

We all ran to the front windows, laughing, running, bumping into each other, laughing some more. The two leaders in the back of the coach shook their heads at our uproar, too tired to care.

Then, without warning, the train stopped—in the middle of nowhere. It wasn't time to stop. We quickly found our seats and held our breath as the conductor passed through our coach searching for anything out of the ordinary.

Dad and his plane were gone. We waited in silence. Each of us silently swore not to say a word, no matter what. We hoped our leaders would keep quiet, too. We didn't want to get kicked off the train. A few minutes later, the train began rolling again.

At dinner that night, Debi and I told Mom all about the crabs, the storm, the mess, and Dad following the train. Then we told her how the train had stopped and the conductor had come back to our coach.

"That's odd," Mom said, looking at Dad curiously. "I wonder what that was all about?"

He looked a little sheepish. "I don't know. I got out of there quick when I saw the train stop. Didn't want anyone to get the tail number off my plane." He smiled.

Mom rolled her eyes and shook her head. With a grin, Dad winked at Debi and me. The three of us shared a secret, and I liked that.

34

Shortly after our move to Balboa, Mom accepted a permanent job as a civilian employee with the U.S. Army. She had often landed temporary office jobs with both the Panama Canal Company and the military, but this time, the job could be hers until she retired. Happiest when she had a job, she was thrilled that something permanent had finally come her way. Soon after, she began taking classes at the college twice a week for her best chance at a promotion. Dad was teaching flying lessons afternoons after work. Two nights a week, he taught ground school and on Wednesday nights, he was involved with church activities.

These changes meant changes for the family. The rule that we'd all sit down for a family dinner when the streetlights came on relaxed. Sometimes we ate together, sometimes we didn't. At times Mom made dinners in a Crockpot or Dad, who loved to cook, would make a meal. Margie and I learned to cook some meals, while at other times, someone would bring home a paper bag filled with *empanadas*. If all else failed, there was "Find Your Own Dinner Night," when leftovers, a can of soup or a bowl of cereal would have to do.

With Mom's new job, we began to enjoy the coveted military privileges that both our parents had been wanting for some time. Now she could shop at the military commissary, meaning more variety and fresher food. Now all of us could shop at the various base exchanges, which were worlds better than the upstairs department of the

Pan Canal Commissary.

"Because Mom has a new job," Dad announced one evening, "we won't be able to go to the States this summer."

We knew we could break up the long summer with a few weekend trips to the beach or we might fly to Costa Rica and spend a couple of days there. For the most part though, we'd be on our own all summer.

Our Girl Scout troop was preparing to march in the Fourth of July parade and this summer, we'd be home. Debi and I couldn't wait for the Canal Zone celebration of our country's Independence Day. Americans living in the Canal Zone prized our U.S. citizenship and loved to demonstrate our patriotism.

For my last year in the Junior Girl Scouts, I was chosen to carry the troop flag. Debi persuaded our leader to let her ride her unicycle on the entire parade route, as she'd practiced a long time and was quite proficient on it. Because our troop had drawn a lucky number and would be marching close to the beginning of the parade, we would have time to disband and watch the rest of the parade go by.

Parades were taken seriously in the Canal Zone and the Fourth of July parade was one of the most important. Our parades had marching bands from the high school and from different military bases. The Army Band, the Marine Band, and the Navy Band each marched and played. The Junior ROTC Honor Guard twirled heavy guns as if they were batons, sometimes tossing the guns back and forth to each other, spinning them in the air.

Local organizations had floats and threw out candy to the crowd. Riders from equine clubs dressed in flashy costumes, with some riders performing tricks on their horses. The Shriners' clowns and minicars created a fun kind of havoc along the parade route.

At times the Panamanian Carnival Queen would ride

Judy carrying the flag in the parade

on her float, stunning and majestic, enthralling Canal Zone daughters with its splendid glamour. The *Bomberos de Panama* Band proudly marched in their red shirts and white pants, their steps keeping perfect time with their unmistakably precise bugles and drums, pleasing American parade watchers, who clapped and cheered for our Panamanian neighbors.

My favorite was the parade's finale. As heavy artillery tanks of the U.S. military barreled down Tavernilla Street past the clubhouse, my insides thrilled with pride at the American soldiers in their field uniforms atop the powerful thundering tanks. As their rumble shook the ground, parade-goers waved in celebration of the men and women ready to fight for our country. With that heavy artillery and our brave armed forces, we felt invincible.

When the parade broke up, many Zonians went to baseball games or picnics at Summit Gardens or Sosa Hill for the afternoon. By evening, Balboa would once more be crowded with people to see the fireworks display.

Dad, Mom, my sisters and I had found a place on the steps of the Administration Building. Between the bottom of the steps and the Goethals Monument, a makeshift bandstand had been set up and lawn chairs and blankets dotted the grassy slope on both sides of the steps.

"There are a hundred and thirteen steps from the Monument to the Admin Building," Margie announced, so Debi and I set out to prove her wrong. We hurried down the steps and then walked back up, counting each one. The hill was steep, so we were more than a little breathless by the time we got back to the top, but Margie was right. One hundred thirteen steps.

Disappointed, we went back to sit down with our family when we saw some friends walking across the elementary school yard and heading up the hill. Debi called out their names, waving to them to sit with us.

We all squeezed together and listened to the 79th Army Band play some jazz pieces, Sousa marches, and patriotic songs until, halfway through the concert, the band director turned to the microphone and said, "If there is any child who wants to come down and lead the music, I am offering you my baton and stepping aside for a short break."

Debi asked Dad, "Is he serious?"

When Dad nodded, she hurried down the steps and joined the line of kids that had formed. One by one, the band director put the baton in a child's hand, and the highly disciplined band followed the new leader.

When Debi's turn came, we watched her step up onto the director's box. She stood tall, raised her arm high, and started the band. As she waved her arm faster, the band players picked up the tempo. She waved her arm even faster, and the music went faster. She slowed her waving to a crawl and the band slowed the music. Then she moved her arm faster again, hoping to catch the band off guard, but they matched her speed beat for beat. When her turn ended, she handed the baton to the next kid in line.

"That was so much fun!" she said, glowing with excitement and out of breath from the hundred-plus stairs.

The band director tapped his baton on his stand, three long taps. The musicians put instruments to their mouths, and a majestic drum roll kicked off "The Star-Spangled Banner." Everyone stood, some placing their hands over their hearts, while others stood at attention in a salute. However we signaled our feelings, everyone there paid reverential tribute to the United States and what our country stands for.

After the Armed Forces band dismantled and packed their instruments into green military trucks, my family and I settled back on the steps to watch the spectacular fireworks. Celebrating the Fourth of July in the Canal Zone rivaled any celebration we'd participated in at Grandma's house in Florida. Like my fellow Zonians, I was surely proud to be an American. I still am.

35

Mom, dressed in a skirt and high heels, drove confidently to the seedy part of Panama City. She and I were on our way to buy her a new car. If the road we were on had a formal name, we didn't know it. It was simply called Automobile Road, because of the different car dealerships and industrial shops that lined the street.

My mother was the type of woman who changed the energy in a room just by walking in. I was used to men falling all over themselves wanting her to notice them.

"She's a captivating woman," Dad would say, not in the least concerned. "Always has been." The salesmen in the car dealership were no exception. We hadn't even reached the outside door before three of them were at Mom's service. The one who spoke the best English beat the other two out. Although we'd lived in Panama for ten years, Mom had never lost her Southern accent, which made me cringe when she tried to speak Spanish.

While the gallant English-speaking Panamanian salesman presented features and options on various models, the other salesmen watched with envy. I wanted to roll my eyes. How could men be so ridiculous?

Quite aware of their silliness, Mom ignored the foolish attention to focus on the business of buying a car. The salesman flattered and smooth-talked her, as he escorted her around the showroom. He didn't even pretend to hide his admiration as she adjusted her skirt over her silky panty-hosed legs climbing in and out of various cars.

Although she charmed him with her smile, the fakeness of the whole transaction was enough to make me want to throw up.

Finally Mom settled on a comfortable blue sedan, and the salesman invited us to finalize the details in the manager's office.

"I'm sorry. My Eenglish ees not good," apologized the handsomely dressed middle-aged sales manager, from behind an ornate mahogany desk, utterly unlike the government-issue desks in the Canal Zone offices. "So Enrique, he weell stay to translate."

I found his apology odd. Quite possibly he could be playing a game. Most successful Panamanian businessmen in the city spoke more than enough English to accomplish their goals. Being bilingual was a prized skill that could mean the difference between success or failure. I couldn't be sure, for after all, we were in the dingy part of a Spanish-speaking city. At any rate, Mom didn't mind Enrique's staying to translate.

Some of the discussion was in English, but for the most part, the two men reverted to Spanish. They both seriously studied the paperwork in front of them, occasionally giving Mom reassuring nods. Naturally, they implied, her best interest was their utmost concern and, of course, they were trying to get her the best deal they could.

Faking boredom, I kept quiet, but I listened to every word. The two men never suspected that I understood Spanish.

Satisfied, Mom signed the contract. Both Enrique and the sales manager raced each other to open the door for her. After the stuffy exchange in the ice-cold air-conditioned office, the heat of the day and fresh air actually felt good.

Irritated drivers in the heavy traffic were freely honking their horns. Mom and I squeezed close together on the sidewalk and took long steps, as it was not unheard of for an impatient driver to use part of the sidewalk to pass another vehicle.

"So," I said to Mom as we crossed to the parking lot, "did you understand what they were saying?"

"I caught a few words, but no, not really. Did you?"

"Pretty much. Something about such a beautiful woman, but really dumb when it comes to buying a car. When they said they were discussing how to get the best contract, they actually were talking about your legs and pretty ankles. Never once did I hear car-related options."

Mom turned on her heels. "C'mon," she said and we walked back inside the dealership. Once again, well-mannered salesmen appeared from nowhere to open doors, graciously wanting to help a lady.

"*Señora*, did you forget something?" the manager politely said.

"May I look at the contract again? I may have written some wrong information."

"Of course."

Mom took the contract from the sales manager and tore the pages in half. Then she tore those halves in half.

The manager's mouth fell open. Before he could say a word, Mom placed the torn pieces of the contract squarely on his desk, turned to the door, smoothly ran her hand down the backside of her skirt and tugged the hem at her knees. She opened the door herself and, with an ever-so-slight exaggeration, swayed her hips and walked out.

"You know," she said, once we had settled back in our old car, "women have much more power than they realize. They just need to know how to tap into it."

As we pulled out of the parking lot, Mom honked the horn to demand her share of space on the busy Panamanian city roads. I couldn't have been more proud of my mother.

36

Kim's family absorbed me as part of their own. Likewise, she became part of my family. In honor of the birth of George Washington, our nation's first president, school was closed on a Monday, granting us a long holiday weekend. Kim invited me to go with her family to their cabin in Cerro Punta. Having enjoyed visits there before, I wished my own parents would buy a cabin in the same mountains, but they didn't. I also wanted Mom and Dad to buy a place at the beach. Panama had so many fun places to live that I dreamed of having a house at each of my favorite places as soon as I was an adult.

"That'll be a lot of houses," Debi said when I told her my dream.

"You can stay at them," I told her.

"I'll have my own houses right next door," she said.

"Great, that works for me."

Our parents preferred to rent cabins or beach houses for holiday weekends. Sometimes, we'd stay at the beaches of Gorgona or Coronado, but it was at the beach of Rio Mar where I learned to relax my body like a limp doll when I took a tumble in the frothy, hard-hitting waves on the Pacific Coast. Eventually the ocean deposited me back onto the shore, even if my bathing suit was weighed down by wet sand.

Sometimes my parents took us to rented cabins in Cerro Punta or the neighboring town of Volcan. At other times, we vacationed with family friends, sharing expenses. As fun as those times were, it was always different going with Kim's family to their cabin.

Cerro Punta, a small, picturesque town in the mountains of Chiriqui Province, is the highest village in the entire country of Panama. It's so high that it's often enveloped by clouds. Especially in the late evenings and early mornings, we'd literally be walking in the clouds. At times we could walk up mountain peaks and look down on the clouds below us.

Driving to Cerro Punta took six hours, the first five on the Interamerican Highway to David, capital of Chiriqui Province. From there we followed a smaller road for the last hour, a roller-coaster ride, dipping through lush green valleys and climbing mountainous curves. Entrances to individual *fincas*—farms—lined the roadside, some entrances with fancy iron gates, while some had just a three-plank wooden gate topped with a single line of barbed wire. Others simply had a sawed-off utility pole with the name of the *finca* painted down the side to mark the entrance.

The *fincas* in Cerro Punta had different specialties. Some specialized in breeding horses or rearing dairy cattle and some specialized in flowers, fruits and vegetables. Most of the produce bought in the Canal Zone and Panama came from this region.

On the way to Kim's family cabin, we passed the *Finca Dracula*, which grew Dracula Orchids. This special variety only wake up at night, never in daylight, to raise their heads and reveal their blossoms. I'd never seen them, though Kim had.

Many homes and cabins around Volcan and Cerro Punta look like Swiss chalets, because Swiss Germans settled here and brought their lifestyle with them. Kim's family cabin was one of the prettiest by far. Six picture windows in the living room and dining area provided a sweeping view of the ice-cold river that flowed past. Three bedrooms were downstairs, with a loft upstairs. Kim and I usually slept in the loft, though once we spent a long weekend in the small travel trailer parked in the side yard.

Each time we arrived, we would unload the car and arrange our clothes in the loft before we headed out. On one trip we had ridden their mini-bike up and down the mountain roads, but the bike was in Balboa for repairs, so we had to walk wherever we wanted to go. Next to the cabin, a rope bridge crossed the river, so we would often walk across the bridge and hike until it was almost dark.

Both Americans and wealthier Panamanians came to Cerro Punta to get away from the Canal Zone's relentless heat and humidity. Here the climate was always the same: sunny days and cool crisp nights, earning this area the nickname, "Land of Eternal Spring."

The people of Cerro Punta are simple and relaxed. For entertainment, neighbors would meet neighbors to talk, play cards, exchange gardening techniques and drink by the fireplaces. One neighbor down the lane, who played the piano, often had a cabin full of people at night, enjoying private concerts or singing familiar songs.

A favorite activity for Kim and me was walking the paved lane after dark. Every night up there, the heavens were so clear and the stars seemed so close, you felt as if you could reach out and cup them in your hand. There was no need for streetlights with the enormous glowing moon and brilliant stars lighting our way.

On the afternoon of our second day over the long holiday, the sun started to feel hot—not uncomfortable, just warm. Kim asked if I wanted to go swimming, meaning in the river by the house. We hadn't brought bathing suits, so we'd have to swim in our shorts and t-shirts.

In the ocean, my preference is to dive right in and get wet all over. "You don't do that here," Kim reminded me, as we climbed down the rocks to the river's edge. Her ritual of describing the procedure for swimming here was always the same.

"First, put your feet in and let them get numb."

That made sense, because that crystal-clear water was icy cold. Once our feet were numb, we edged out further until the water reached our mid-calves. I sucked in my breath and waited until my heart began beating again. Then we moved further into the river until the water was up to our knees.

"I dare you to dive from here," Kim said, shivering.

I was too cold to answer. Once our legs were numb from our toes to our knees, we inched in further until we were waist-deep. It seemed to take us forever to go numb from the knees to the waist, but after that our bodies accepted the inevitable.

Kim looked over at me. "You ready?"

I nodded and we dove in at the same time, both came up and swam to the edge of the river as quickly as possible. We grabbed our towels, cursed our stupidity, and went right back into the water before we had a chance to defrost, unwilling to start the procedure all over again. By the time our bodies were completely numb and we were beginning to enjoy the swim, it was time to get out.

On Sunday, the last full day of this trip, after Kim and I had gone hiking, swum in the river, visited neighbors, read comic books, and played endless board games, we looked for something different to do. First we crossed the swinging rope bridge and walked up the mountainside, then wandered down a lane to the establishment of a local *hombre* who rented horses for trail rides.

"I have a few dollars, how about a ride?" I suggested.

"I forgot you know how to ride," Kim said.

"Well, it's been a while." I was starting to wish I hadn't suggested it.

Technically I knew how to ride, although even when Margie had her horse in Gamboa, I had rarely done it. On vacation Dad had occasionally rented horses for us to have an hour's ride, but the truth was I still wasn't comfortable on a horse and often felt I didn't know what I was doing.

With just enough money to rent one horse, Kim and I would have to ride double. There was no saddle, so the owner threw a thick blanket over the mare's back for us to sit on. No reins either, so I took hold the rope instead and Kim climbed on behind me.

When I pressed in my heels the mare didn't move. I leaned into her and once more nudged my heels. The mare stood still. Firmly, I tried again. Nothing.

"¿Qué pasa con el caballo?" I asked the owner standing a few feet away.

"Nada, señorita, No hay problema con el caballo."

How could there not be a problem with the creature? My horsemanship was limited, but I'd never had a problem getting one to take at least a step or two.

The owner said she was stubborn and I needed to use much more force. So I used my legs to prod the mare's side, jabbed harder with my heels, made clicking sounds, and moved my body forward—but the mare wouldn't move.

I'd reached the end of my equine skills. The owner grabbed a switch from a tree and handed it to me. I shook my head to say no, I'm not using a switch.

"Sí, señorita. Date es waat de caballo needs."

I held the switch, but I couldn't bring myself to use it. Grabbing another switch, the owner cracked it on the thick-skinned rump and the mare bolted.

Kim held tight to my waist, while I held the rope even tighter. We were headed straight for the river.

I tugged on the reins, urging the mare to go left, only to be ignored. She ran right to the river, put her head down, and abruptly stopped, trying to throw us off into the icy water.

Astonished, Kim and I clamped our legs onto her tighter as I urged the mare to turn around and walk. Again, she refused to move. We might as well have been on a statue. I took all of the steps I had taken before. Nothing.

Finally, I lifted the switch in a threatening manner so she could see it and *that* caught the mare's attention. She turned then and cantered down the path as if she'd been doing the right thing all along.

I felt pleased to have mastered the critter. Soon the ride became almost enjoyable, so Kim and I began to relax. However, that mare was craftier than I'd thought. As soon as she felt us relax, she took off again in a zig-zag pattern, ignoring all my commands.

Faster and faster she moved, until she was at a full-on gallop, with Kim's arms tightened around my waist again. This time, when the crazy mare headed for a tree with a low-hanging limb, I leaned forward to press my head against the mare's neck. However, Kim didn't see the limb and didn't duck, so she was caught squarely across her chest, which blew us both off onto the ground.

Stunned, all the air was knocked out of me. For a moment I was in a void of darkness and silence until I managed to squeak, "Kim, are we dead?"

"No, Judy, we aren't dead."

"I think we might be."

"We're not dead, Judy."

"How do you know? Have you ever been dead before?"

Kim reached over to pinch my arm, "Can you feel that?"

When I said, "Yes," she said, "That's how I know we're not dead."

We lay there motionless on the hard ground for a few minutes. Then Kim asked, "Are you hurt?"

"I've started to get feeling back in my body, so I don't think anything is broken. What about you?"

"I don't think I've broken any bones either."

Cautiously we started to stand up.

The mare was nearby, grazing calmly, watching us with one eye. We ignored her and walked to the rope bridge. I wanted my money back, but the mare's owner was nowhere to be seen.

"Forget about it," Kim said. "Let's go play Monopoly."

We both had a new limp in our walk.

37

The summer between my ninth and tenth grades, our whole family came back from home leave in Florida two weeks after school had started. The *Cristobal*, now used mostly as a cargo ship, carried few passengers. Gone were the former glory days of party cruises on the same ship. Our voyage was quiet, peaceful, and monotonous.

Once we docked and disembarked, Dad allowed Margie, Debi, and me to take the train home, while he, Mom, and Connie waited for the car and luggage to be unloaded. From the train station, we three girls walked home and called all of our friends, excited to talk about our trip and catch up on neighborhood gossip.

Later that evening, I showed Kim my new clothes from the States. I'd be going to Balboa High, while she remained at Curundu for her ninth grade. For two years she and I had ridden the same bus and sat on the same bench seat, seen each other in the school hallways, and gone to each other's homes after school.

Now I would wait at the bus stop with other high-school kids from the neighborhood. I knew them quite well, but when the bus came, I took an empty seat to myself.

After my typing class I hurried to my locker, grabbed my paper-bag lunch, and stuffed it into my purse. Then I squeezed through the crowd of students going up and down the stairs. Once I reached the basement, I stopped and self-consciously surveyed the cafeteria. Rows and rows of tables and chairs lined the back half of the room.

The front half contained vending and soda machines, a few large commercial microwaves, a table with condiments and silverware, and the hot-food serving area. For those buying a lunch, the line was long.

I saw plenty of people I knew, but no empty seats beside them. Most of my classmates were too busy talking with each other or eating their lunch to pay any attention to me. I hated feeling awkward and looked forward to the time when my school life would settle into a routine.

Spotting my long-time friend, Eve, at the room's far end near the exit stairway, I headed toward her. Fewer people sat in that part of the cafeteria, so it was quieter and less hectic. Also, from here we could see who was leaving with whom. After Eve introduced me to our other tablemates, I opened my lunch bag and took out my ham sandwich and tangerine.

About a month later, Carol Carroll joined our lunch table and sat across from me. Eve had noticed her standing alone and characteristically invited her to our table. We started chatting and hit it off right away. In only a few minutes, I learned her story.

Her father was an Air Force officer and her family had been transferred from the States to Howard Air Force Base. Miserable about leaving the States to come to the Canal Zone, she was tired of all the changes in her life. Carol's mother had been a single mom in Alabama when she'd started dating Major Carroll. They'd soon married, making Carol, along with her older brother and younger sister, part of a military family. I knew that was a drastically different life for someone who until then had had a more typical American one. Major Carroll had adopted the three kids and given them his name. Carol Anderson had become Carol Carroll.

The romance of the story drew me in like a novel. The fact that her first name and last name were now the same I absolutely loved. For her, though, her unusual name bothered her. She said people looked at her funny whenever she told them.

"It makes you unique," I told her as we walked back to class. "My name is a boring, everyday name. But yours ..."

The last thing Carol wanted was to be unique. She wanted to be the same as everyone else. She wanted to fit in. Okay, if that was going to happen, she would first have to take care of her excessive makeup, I decided.

I couldn't help but stare and wonder at Carol's teased hair and colorful makeup. First, dark-blue eye shadow in the crease of her eyes, with a lighter blue shadow on the lids. As if that weren't enough, a lighter pale-blue shadow on the brow bone, and framing the whole creation was blue eyeliner. Carol's mascara-darkened eyelashes were unnaturally long, separated and precisely curled. Her lips looked large with a bold-red lipstick that intensified her heightened rose-colored cheekbones. She must have gotten up at the crack of dawn to get ready for school.

I barely wore makeup. Sometimes, I wore some eye shadow and a little mascara, though I usually didn't bother. My cheeks were often rosy from the sun and my eyelashes were naturally long and dark, so I didn't feel the need to add to them. Anyway, wire-rim John Lennon eyeglasses went on top of any makeup I might wear.

With her atypical name, exotic makeup, Alabama accent, and trendy clothes fresh from the States, Carol Carroll certainly did stand out.

We compared class schedules to find that our only similar class was chorus, but that it was not at the same period. None of our other classes were even in the same building. Disappointed, we decided to get together to talk before school and during lunch.

A few weeks later, Carol and I were walking up the stairs from the cafeteria heading for our usual spot by the tree across the street to wait for the bell signaling our afternoon classes. By then, Carol had toned down her makeup, though she still teased out her bangs in a poufy sort of way. Thick platform shoes and wide flared jeans were also reminders that she hadn't lived in the Canal Zone long.

"You know, Judy, I really hate living here," Carol said. "I miss my old life. I want to go home so much. I want things to be like they used to be."

I was surprised. "How can you hate living here?" I'd never before met anyone who hated the Canal Zone. When we had visitors from the States they always told us we were lucky to live in such a paradise. While I certainly looked forward to visiting the States in the summer, nothing beat coming home. I liked this way of life, and I liked the people. I couldn't imagine living anywhere else. Sure, I planned to go away for college, but after that I intended to raise my own kids right here and have the same life I'd always had.

Carol kept talking. "All I do after school is go home and do homework. There's hardly anything to watch on TV. There's no mall. The movies are old by the time they get here. There's nothing to do." That air of sadness never seemed to leave Carol.

Even so, comparing the Canal Zone to the States, she was right. We had no fast-food places, no variety of stores to browse or shop, no mall, amusement park or fancy tourist attractions. There wasn't even much change of seasons, only two—rainy and dry.

Although living on the military bases had some advantages and for the most part, military kids and Canal Zone kids did a lot of the same things, there was a difference. Military kids were temporary and might move at any time, while Canal Zone kids were permanent and shared an unseen fraternity. Carol felt that distinction.

"The way I see it," I told her, "you have four years of

living here. Actually, three if you go to college in the States after high school. At the very most, your dad will be transferred in four years. Now, you can either stay miserable and hate life for the next four years, or you can hang out with me. I can show you how to have fun living here."

I watched as my new friend considered my words. Finally she looked up. "You're right. Let's have some fun."

Friday afternoon, the dismissal bell rang promptly at 2:15. Instead of crossing the street over to Goethals Monument where the Pan Canal school buses parked, I walked to the side road between the school and the gym where military dependents boarded their school buses so I could meet Carol there.

The bus driver nodded to acknowledge that I was a new face on the bus and I felt his eyes on my back until I sat next to Carol. I watched ROTC students outside line up for their afternoon drills and bits and pieces of conversation concerning tonight's football game drifted from every seat on the bus.

When the bus crossed Thatcher Ferry Bridge, I assumed my best tour-guide voice for Carol's benefit. "This is the Bridge of Americas. It connects Central America and South America."

She looked out the window at a cargo ship going through the Canal. "So what?"

I shrugged. "I don't know. I hear my dad tell people that."

The MP waved us onto Howard Air Force Base, where the bus wound through enlisted-personnel family quarters to let some students off before continuing up the hill to the officers' quarters. Carol's house was near the top of the hill, with an impressive view of Panama City and the bay.

After I met her mom, brother, and sister, I told her mom I would like Carol to spend the night at my house.

When her mom agreed, Carol packed an overnight bag and came with me to catch a Canal Zone bus to Balboa and retrace our route.

"When you learn how to use the bus system," I told her, "you have more freedom than you can imagine. Sure, having a car would be awesome, but right now I depend on the bus."

The bus headed down the bridge ramp. The driver braked for the stoplight at the end of the bridge, and I called out, "*Parada*," meeting his eyes in the rear-view mirror. He stopped and pulled the lever to open the doors.

"This isn't a bus stop," Carol said as we stepped off.

"It doesn't have to be. Why go all the way to the bus stop when we can get off right here? It's closer to my house." We walked down the sidewalk along Amador Road.

I took Carol up the back steps to our kitchen so she could meet my mom and dad. I noticed my parents' eyes shift when I introduced them to Carol, who wasn't like other friends I'd brought home.

They told me later they were concerned that Carol might be wild. Her being fresh from the States, wearing teased hair and platform shoes with stylish clothes had certainly made an impression. Could mean trouble with a capital T, they said. Even though I told them she was nothing like that, they weren't convinced.

Mom said, "What's wrong with Kim?"

"Nothing's wrong with Kim."

Kim had been my best friend for three years and would always be my friend. She still had one more year in Curundu and had made new good friends there. I was now going to Balboa High School and I had met Carol.

I no longer had the bedroom next to the kitchen, but was now sleeping in a room underneath the house. Though it was common for Canal Zone families to convert maid's quarters to bedrooms for teenagers, we used our maid's room for storage. After Dad enclosed part of the underneath to make two bedrooms with a connecting doorway, Debi and I moved downstairs.

Our "suite" included the outside utility bathroom complete with exposed pipes, unfinished cement blocks, and an occasional spider web in the joists overhead. Our bedroom doors lead directly to the outside. From there it was only a few steps to the back cement stairs to the kitchen and the rest of the main house. So while technically our rooms were part of the house, Debi and I enjoyed the distance from the rest of the family.

When Carol and I went down to my bedroom, I asked her if she really wanted to walk all over Balboa and back home again wearing her impractical shoes.

She said, "I didn't bring any others."

I tossed over a pair of my *huaraches*. "Here."

When she put them on, her jeans scraped the ground the same way as mine. I figured it would take time to convince her to stop teasing her bangs and be comfortable with the wash-and-wear hairstyle typical for Zonian girls.

An intercom connected our bedrooms to my parents' room and just then its buzzer sounded. I pushed the button.

"Yeah?" I said into the machine.

Dad's voice broke through the static. "If you want a ride to the post office, I'm leaving now."

So Carol and I climbed into the station wagon and rode with Dad to town. While he checked the mailbox, she and I walked through Steven's Circle and headed over to the stadium. The half-time show was about over and our school's two teams, the Bulldogs and the Red Machine, would be coming back on the field at any minute.

Carol and I squeezed into the crowd streaming back to their seats for the second half of the game. She said, "You don't think it's odd that one high school has two varsity football teams that compete against each other?"

"Maybe," I said, "but that way, we have more games and more competition."

Besides the two Balboa High School football teams, there were only three others: Canal Zone Junior College, Cristobal High (from the Other Side) and Curundu Junior High.

Carol still couldn't make sense of it. "With two teams from the same school, how do you know who to cheer for?"

"That's easy. I cheer for the team with the cutest guys."

Carol had started to take a seat on the bleachers when I gave her a nudge. "There's Paul," I said, pointing to the sidelines. "Let's go stand by him."

Paul smiled when we wedged in next to him, reaching into his pocket to hand each of us a rose apple from the tree by his house. I bit right into mine, enjoying the fruit's fine crispy white meat, but Carol sniffed the fruit and hesitated, saying it smelled like the rosewater perfume her grandma wore.

"Well," Paul said, "it does sort of taste like the perfume."

She put the apple in her purse, saying she'd eat it later. Carol didn't want to try something new in front of us, not wanting to hurt our feelings if she didn't like the taste.

After the game, Paul walked with us over to the bowling alley that was full of milling Zonian teens. A few hoped for a ride to a party in some nameless clearing in the jungle, while others positioned themselves to be seen and noticed. Close to ten o'clock, a crowd of us headed over to the movie theater for the Owl Show. I looked around for Kim to see if she had made it, but she wasn't there, probably went to the Diablo Theater for a better movie.

At the theater, people had already lined up outside, so in another few minutes, the line would stretch down the sidewalk. With people to talk to in line, the wait passed quickly. We bought our tickets and walked through to the inner lobby, bypassing the concession stand to head straight into the theater and find seats near the center. I looked around as discreetly as I could to see who else was there and waved at a few people behind us.

At midnight, the Owl Show ended and the theater's side doors opened. With most of the town's lights off, the empty streets and shadowy buildings appeared ominous.

Carol shivered as we went out. "It's like a ghost town," she said, "a little unnerving."

A few movie-goers climbed into waiting cars and left, as Carol and I joined a group of kids headed toward Amador Road, while other groups walked down the Prado or up Tavenilla Street. After we passed the police station, our group broke up to go their separate ways, leaving Carol and me on our own.

Amador Road was dark, deserted, and looming. "It's exactly one mile from the police station to my house," I told Carol. We walked fast, looking back over our shoulders repeatedly. Concentrating on getting home, neither of us wanted to talk about the blood-curdling scenes we had just watched on the movie screen.

Safe in my bedroom, Carol and I both breathed sighs of relief. Debi was spending the night at a friend's house, so I took her bed and gave Carol mine.

"You know," Carol said as I turned off the lights. "I could come to like living here."

"Here's to good friends." I raised my hand like I had a glass of wine. Then I crawled into Debi's bed.

38

Living in Panama often brought us a feeling of isolation and detachment from Americans who lived in the States. Zonians barely paid attention to the filtered local news or the worn-out shows that no longer even merited rerun time in the States. Trends and fashions were outdated by the time we even knew they existed.

Of course, many fashions were seasonal and since we had two seasons, rainy and dry, we had no reason to care about fall or winter clothes. As our Stateside friends and relatives progressed to newer and fresher ideas, we were seemingly backward and out of step with the world.

However, during my tenth-grade year, the Armed Forces television station in the Canal Zone, SCN, entered a new era in broadcasting, including starting an hour earlier. Now at three in the afternoon, the screen projected a picture of the U.S. flag with *The Star Spangled Banner* as recorded background music. This was followed by a few public-service announcements, *Sesame Street*, *Cartoon Carnival*, and a heavy-breasted female fitness instructor demonstrating exercise techniques. Precisely at 4:50 P.M., the world of many Zonians came to a halt, as we watched *General Hospital* for twenty minutes. The absence of commercials meant that our television shows were compressed and started at odd times. It also meant that the programs didn't last long, leaving us plenty of time to "do our chores and finish homework," as Mom would say.

At first, Mom was disappointed with the change.

When we stayed at Grandma's during the summer, *The Edge of Night* and *As the World Turns* were her "stories." "Honestly," she complained, "of all the soaps to be brought down, *General Hospital* is the worst. It might have been decent a few years ago, but now it's pitiful. No way am I getting involved in that soap."

Carol, on the other hand, loved the show, which had been her favorite in Alabama. "*General Hospital* is the only normal American thing about living here," she said. As far as she was concerned, the program was the one saving grace when her family moved to Howard Air Force Base.

But Carol found that watching the soap opera in the Canal Zone wasn't the same as it had been in Alabama. The show ran several months behind current episodes in the States. Zonians who returned from TDY or leave in the States knew what was going to happen, so their phone lines buzzed with upcoming *General Hospital* news.

I started watching the show with Carol and soon was hooked myself. Before long, my entire family became followers, Mom the biggest addict of us all. We wondered if Steve and Audrey would ever find happiness. We were captivated by Dr. Lesley's discovery of her daughter, Laura, whom the good doctor thought had died years ago. We were devastated when Laura left Scotty for Luke—until we fell in love with Luke as well.

With the arrival of *General Hospital*, our sense of detachment from the States began to change. Zonians began to feel more in touch with other Americans. Our episodes may have been a few months old, but at least we were living in the same year.

But Stateside, *General Hospital* was failing miserably in the ratings wars and word got out that it would soon be cancelled. Canal Zone residents may very well have saved that show, for it was Zonians who got their visiting

Stateside friends hooked on the show. It was Zonians who began subscribing to the new soap-opera digests, hungry for more information about their one and only soap. And it was Zonians on leave in the States who religiously watched *General Hospital,* even when there were many competing shows running at the same time. Indeed, this small group of Americans were the show's most loyal fans.

39

About this time, Dad had a hot-dog stand shipped down for his Boy Scout troop to run and earn money, since there were almost no jobs for Canal Zone teenagers. Unless you had a good babysitting clientele, which I sometimes did or other little jobs, Zonian kids had none. There were a few lifeguard or movie-usher jobs, but only a handful of kids found part-time employment. Dad figured that his Boy Scouts could run a hot-dog stand and earn money for their camping trips, *cayucos* and other expenses.

At first, the plan went rather well, until the Scouts found things they would rather do than spend a Saturday selling hot dogs and sodas.

"Let me run the hot-dog stand," I volunteered after another Friday night of Dad calling Scouts to see if anyone was available.

"You can't."

Dad explained how private retail and food businesses were not allowed to operate in the Canal Zone. Fund raisers were allowed, which was how Dad had obtained a special permission certificate.

So together, Dad and I hatched a plan. I'd run the hot-dog stand as a stand-in and give a percentage to his scouting program. I would give Dad a percentage to pay for the concession stand he'd bought and I'd pay Mom back for the hot dogs, buns, soda, and ice she would buy at the commissary. I'd split the rest with whoever worked with me.

Carol and Judy working at the hot dog stand on Steven's Circle

On a good Saturday, my partner and I ended up with about twenty dollars each. On a slow Saturday, we were lucky to split five or six dollars. Many times, Carol worked with me. Some Saturdays, when my friends and I went to the beach, I didn't work, but on Saturdays when Carol and I wanted to work, we rolled the hot-dog cart from the back of the commissary across to Stevens Circle, where we set up next to the road. While we were getting everything ready with water boiling in one of the compartments,

Mom would drive around to the nearest parking spot, so we wouldn't have far to carry the groceries. Dad's job was to go to the ice house and fill up several coolers with crushed ice. Once we were set up, Mom went home.

Carol and I sold hot dogs to people passing through the plaza on their way to the post office or commissary. At times, Cuna Indian women sold their *molas* on the circle or other Zonians set up a blanket and sold pet rocks, ceramics, or paintings. At other times, Carol and I would be the only vendors there.

Some customers would drive by our hot-dog stand and call out their order, then drive around the circle and come back so one of us could carry the order right to their car—kind of a Flintstone way of doing things, but it worked. Some time after two o'clock, Carol and I would return the hot-dog stand to the far side of the commissary, steam-clean it, and roll it into the storage room until the next time.

On some Saturday nights, if Carol spent the night with me, we walked a short distance from our house to the Balboa Yacht Club to meet with friends who were usually drinking or smoking at the downstairs bar. At other times, we would sit on the bank of the Canal, watch the small boats bob up and down, enjoy the tropical breeze and talk about nothing of any consequence.

If we could catch a ride, sometimes Carol and I would go to the Pub, an old railway coach crudely transformed into a bar, with a wooden porch added as a stage for local bands to play a mixture of Reggaeton music with a Canal Zone calypso twist.

It didn't matter to me or my friends that I didn't drink or smoke, since Carol and I were there to dance in a reverie under the huge starlit Panama sky.

40

I was walking through Balboa High School's breezeway to my chorus class in the theater building, when Bobby asked me to the Junior-Senior prom. I seemed to have known Bobby for ages—couldn't even remember when I met him. He had always been a part of the fabric of my life in Balboa. I could hardly wait to tell Carol! I was pleased that Bobby had asked me, though we'd be going as friends, not dates. I was comfortable with him, no strings attached.

The prom was over a month away, so I had plenty of time to get a dress. Mom and I wasted no time going to the city to buy material. Like many Canal Zone moms, she sewed most of my dresses. Panama City had fancy dress shops, but they were out of our budget. It would take too long to order anything from a catalog and there was always a chance it wouldn't fit. The second floor of the Canal Zone commissary sold clothing, but it was rare when anyone could find anything stylish, the right size, or even wearable there. It was fine for basics like jeans, t-shirts, underwear, socks, and shorts, but you'd have to be very lucky to find something suitable in the few formal gowns that hung in a back corner.

Mom was a proficient seamstress. Every summer in Florida, she usually signed up for sewing classes and learned new techniques. "It's a matter of survival," she said. Of course it was, with four daughters.

Many times we returned home to Panama with one suitcase packed with yards of fabric to add to her collection of patterns and material gleaned from downtown Panama City's small, suffocating, tucked-away shops.

With her friends, Mom traded Simplicity and McCall patterns the way avid sports fans trade baseball cards. She welcomed an excuse to go the fabric stores and thumb through oversized, finger-worn pattern books and search for newer, fresher cloth.

I chose a creamy beige cotton for my prom dress. We found an ivory bodice and lace edging for trim. Mom took my measurements and adjusted her dress form to my size, then spent a Saturday afternoon cutting out the dress and pinning the pieces together. Since she wouldn't need me for fittings, Carol and I took the bus to Dee's house in Albrook.

In my purse, I had a box with two 14-karat gold studs I'd picked up at the Corazal Base Exchange, because I was going to get my ears pierced. The week before, in school, Dee had excitedly announced to Carol and me that she'd had her ears pierced. Her small gold studs glimmered at the center of her earlobes. I wanted mine done, too.

Dad had told me months ago in no uncertain terms that if God wanted girls to have holes in their ears, He would have put them there Himself. I argued that the Cuna Indian women had their noses pierced, so they could wear a gold hoop there, and Dad didn't object to that. He countered that Cuna Indians were a completely different matter and I was welcome to wear a gold hoop in my nose and live on the San Blas Islands with the Cuna Indians, if I felt that's where I belonged.

Dee's father had told her basically the same thing, except he'd left out the part about living with the Cuna Indians. So Dee had bought stud earrings from the base exchange and had her next-door neighbor, Karen, pierce her ears. Her father didn't even know it, because Dee's hair covered her ears. I decided that would be my plan as well.

"Are you ready?" Dee asked when Carol and I arrived. I nodded, eager to get it done. Karen's lieutenant husband had been transferred to Albrook from the States a few months before and we walked to her house to find her watching the Armed Forces TV station urging military personnel and their dependents to visit the Perlas Islands for fun and recreation. Then we heard the SCN announcer say, "While living in Central America, there are phrases you should know."

Karen stopped. "Oh, wait. This is what I've been waiting for. I have to see this."

Words in both Spanish and English flashed on the small black-and-white screen as the announcer distinctively pronounced each of the words. Karen wrote the Survival Spanish tips in her notebook, looked back at us, then cut off the TV with a smile. "Let's do it."

Two minutes later, I was in Karen's kitchen holding an ice cube to my earlobe while she stood at the sink, sterilizing a sewing needle with a match flame. She'd already inked a dot on each of my earlobes, for the location of each hole, while Carol wiped alcohol on the posts of my new gold studs.

"You ready?" Karen asked.

I nodded. She pushed the needle through, then the gold stud, and fastened the little post behind my ear. That was easy. I didn't feel a thing.

Dee held up a hand mirror, "One ear down. One to go."

I admired the pretty gold stud and loved how it looked. Excited, I put ice on the other earlobe, while Karen sterilized the needle again.

The second piercing didn't go as smoothly. Holding the ice cube lower than the marked spot, I had numbed the wrong place. As the needle probed my flesh I felt every teeny nerve and heard tiny unnerving noises as it pierced all the way through. Then a drop of blood seeped out, surprising us all. We hadn't expected blood. My first ear hadn't bled. Dee's ears hadn't bled.

At first we were quiet, then Karen quickly rubbed alcohol on my earlobe and forced the gold post through. I let out my breath, and we waited to see what would happen next, like if I fainted. Nothing happened.

A short time later Carol, Dee and I left, and Karen went back to her TV to wait for the next SCN Survival Spanish tip. Dee pushed my hair back and looked at my new ornaments and red earlobes.

"Becoming a lady can be painful," she said, letting the hair fall back over my ears, "but we do what we have to do."

For days afterward, I cleaned my earlobes religiously with rubbing alcohol and was spared any infection. For almost a week, I managed to hide my newly pierced ears from Mom and Dad until one day when I forgot, pulled my hair back into a ponytail, and sat down at the dinner table.

As expected, Dad was "duly disappointed." Mom said she hoped I knew what I was doing. Margie shook her head, and Connie talked about second grade. Debi thought I was cool. *Way to go, Judy,* her eyes said. She wanted her ears pierced right away, until she saw Dad's hard stare, but she didn't fool me. I knew she was calculating a way to get her own ears pierced as soon as possible.

Weather-wise, the day of the Junior-Senior Prom was like any other Saturday—hot, damp, and sticky. Mom had finished my long dress two days before, and it still hung on her dress form. She'd spent hours sewing the ivory lace with tiny hand stitches to the scoop neckline. As I fingered the sleeves where she'd painstakingly sewn intricate matching buttons into the lace itself, my excitement bubbled over. What a beautiful dress!

Then Bobby called to say he might not be able to get his

mom's car. Would I be terribly disappointed if we went in his truck? It might be old and rusty, he said, but it was reliable. He must have known my silence meant disappointment, so he said he'd do everything possible to borrow his mom's car.

Mom had some last-minute advice. "Always be a lady," she said. "You can tell Bobby what you'd like to eat, but let him order the dinner." When she noticed my surprise, she smiled. "It's a simple gesture. Save your independent streak for something that really matters."

Just before dark, to my relief, Bobby pulled up in his mother's white Buick and came to the front door. With the red-carnation corsage he gave me pinned to my dress and the polite small talk with my parents over, Bobby and I left. After we were in the car, he cracked me up with his low appreciative whistle.

"I thought we'd go to the Union Club for dinner," he said, heading toward Panama City.

"Really!" I was impressed.

El Club Unión was an exclusive members-only club where wealthy Panamanians dined, played cards, and made important business deals. Bobby drove underneath the towering red archway to leave the car with the parking attendant. Braided crimson rope lined the brilliantly lit entrance, where several uniformed doormen greeted Bobby and me and ushered us through. We sat by a terrace with a full view of the Canal's entrance. Through the windows, we could see a few ships waiting in the outer anchorage for their turn to transit, once they had an experienced Canal pilot on board to assume full command.

I followed Mom's advice, telling Bobby what I wanted to eat and letting him tell the waiter. I thought it was stupid, but I could play the game.

We finished off an elegant meal complete with a dessert of *Tres Leches* cake, and after he tipped the parking attendant, drove on to Curundu Junior High. The Prom, like most of our school dances, took place in the cafeteria.

The decorating committee had transformed the drab school area into a warm and inviting ballroom. Blue and white streamers hung from the rafters, and the normally glaring lights were dimmed. White linen cloths covered the tables under centerpieces of paper flowers that propped up cards printed with black numbers. Bobby had reserved our table weeks before, and we looked for Table Number 12.

Soon the tables were all filled and the prom was in full swing. At first, Bobby and I kept to our seats, just people-watching but then got up for a slow-dance to *My Eyes Adored You,* interpreted by the band's Latin beat. We followed that by Canal Zone versions of the *Salsa* and *Merengue.* When the band started strumming the first measures of *La Bamba,* the cafeteria resounded with cheers as partiers scraped back their chairs to hurry onto the dance floor. And then for a couple of hours my classmates and Bobby and I danced to both Latin and American music.

A little after eleven P.M., as we left the cafeteria and returned to the car, Bobby handed me a small purse full of change. "This is from my mom," he said. "You want to try our luck at the slot machines?"

Oh, yeah! I was definitely in. Panama City had plenty of casinos to choose from. We headed for *Hotel El Panama* on *Via España,* an opulent hotel in the heart of the city with an active night life. I had come there at times with my parents to listen to Lucho play the organ.

The smoky haze swirling amid the intricate carved designs on the creamy plaster columns created a surreal ambiance. In the casino, we scanned the slot machines lined up along the ornate walls. Well-dressed men and their scantily dressed companions hovered around the roulette tables and card games, as tuxedoed waiters circled the room collecting scattered wine and champagne glasses. In my prom dress, with my newly pierced ears, I felt I was floating in this sophisticated world.

The nickel machines attracted us first, then the dime and quarter slots. We won a little, lost more. We spotted other prom-dressed Zonians across the room, winning and losing, too.

Bobby wanted to play until all our money was gone, but I insisted that we leave before that and put the unspent coins back in the purse for Bobby to return to his mother.

After midnight, only a few cars were on Panama's streets. We were back at my house in minutes.

"I had a great time," I said when he switched off the Buick's engine. Always the gentleman, Bobby walked me to the door and gave me a hug. I had just enjoyed a very happy evening.

41

Carol spent a Friday night at my house and Bobby agreed to drive us to Goofy Falls on Saturday. It was a fun place to swim, and I didn't go as often as I'd have liked, as you needed a car to get there.

In the morning, Carol and I got up early to pack lunch. Scrounging around the kitchen, we found little to bring. Mom shopped every other Thursday, and this happened to be the off week. So it was peanut-butter-and-jelly sandwiches, bananas from the tree in our yard, a half bag of potato chips, a handful of *Maria* cookies wrapped in tin foil, and Kool-Aid in a Thermos jug. With our packed lunch and rolled towels, we sat outside on the front steps of the house to wait. Minutes later, Bobby's familiar Ford truck pulled up. The food went into the bed of the truck and then the three of us squeezed onto the bench seat.

Goofy Falls was an hour's drive from Panama City, past Tocumen Airport and up into the hills. The slate-gray two-lane highway wound through farmland, rolling green hills and sprawling acres of indistinguishable vegetation. We were soon beyond all the stores, with almost no houses and certainly no telephones.

Bobby parked at the roadside atop a hill. A small patch of dirt on the shoulder of the road just big enough to park three or four cars told us we were nearly at Goofy Falls. We could see all the way to Tocumen, Panama City and the Pacific Ocean.

We were headed across the road to a big field

Loving Goofy Falls

surrounded by barbed wire. Bobby grabbed the Thermos, Carol grabbed the towels, and I grabbed lunch. Propped idly under a tree was an old Panamanian man with a shotgun beside him. Bobby gave him a few dollars and the *viejo* nodded. We would give him another dollar or two when we got back and found the truck intact.

Seeing Carol's confused look, I explained. "He'll watch the truck. If he didn't, someone might steal the tires or battery." She seemed reassured.

We scooted under the barbed wire and found the path. We had maybe a hundred yards to go, but the cows in the field always made me nervous. When Bobby hollered a loud "MOO!" it didn't faze them. Keeping their large cow eyes on us, they went on munching grass.

The pasture led into a thick forest, where after a short distance, the path became a rocky trail with big boulders on each side. Before we reached the falls, we could hear the noise of it crashing onto large rocks.

We three were the only ones there, though more people were likely to come. Sometimes other Zonians made their way to the place or a few GIs might show up, but for the most part, secluded Goofy Falls was private.

To look at, the falls weren't impressive, nothing like Niagara or Angel Falls, but they were truly powerful. Just being close to such a noisy torrent was energizing and great fun. Beyond a lush wall of trees, we set our lunch and towels on one of the flat rocks near the rushing stream. I'd worn my bathing suit under my t-shirt and shorts so I took them off and laid them on my towel.

I was eager to start playing in the water, but Carol was nervous.

"Suppose someone gets hurt," she said, "or something happens? We're up here far from any kind of help."

That thought never crossed my mind.

"Oh, come on in and don't worry about it. We'll be fine."

The falls had two upper pools and one below. I jumped from a rock into the cool fresh water of the largest one. On one side, a torrent of water poured down from the cliff's highest point, where several smaller chutes of water add-ed to the swirling mass. To the side, still smaller streams poured down to the third pool, and from there the river continued downstream.

I swam to the far side of the swimming hole where a fat twisted rope hung from a tree branch. I grabbed the rope, swung out to the middle of the water and dropped in. Bobby followed me and Carol shook off her reluctance and jumped in after him.

When I tired of the rope, I climbed the rocks to a pool higher up, slipped into the water at a relatively calm spot and swam behind the strong swirling current that fed the largest part of the falls.

On the far side, a rush of water formed a natural slide down to the second pool, with several boulders at the top to shield it from the main force of the water. I positioned myself atop the slide, and when I was ready, let go of the rock I was hanging on to and slid down to the lower pool, where the force of the water beat me down to the depths.

I knew not to panic or let the current push me against the sharp rocks that framed the basin. Once I cleared that part of the falls, I drifted over to the smaller, gentler chute to slide down to calmer water, climbed out and walked up the rocks to do it all over again.

Bobby and Carol refused to go behind the main water-fall. While I didn't want to admit it, I was a little nervous each time I did it.

In the second pool again, I flattened myself against the cliff and gradually inched my way around the smoother rocks at the edge of the falls. There was a space of a foot or so between the point where the water tumbled off the precipice and the supporting wall. Halfway across the wall, a small shelf protruded from the bedrock. Working my way into that hidden space, I sat and watched from behind the main torrent, amazed and exhilarated by the awesome force plunging only inches from my nose.

As soon as I gathered my courage, I dove under the falls, once more feeling the thundering water pound my body and render me helpless, tumbling me like a rag in a washing machine. When a surge pushed me out into the calmer water, I swam to the side and climbed out.

We hadn't been there long, when three guys showed up. Bobby knew one of them from school. They waved to us and set out their towels up a ways from ours; the unmistakable sweet smell of Panama Red filtered downstream.

By midday, a few more people had arrived. As soon as that bunch went to the rope and began swinging out and splashing into the water, our private swimming hole was suddenly noisy and crowded.

Bobby, Carol, and I got out, ate our lunch, and soaked in some sunshine. Bobby said he wanted to check out something in the trees. Carol and I knew he went to pee. We giggled and lay back on our towels. Too soon it would be time to go home. It seemed like the most perfect day.

42

It was a Saturday night when Bobby came for Carol and me in his Ford pickup to go to a party at Tom's house in Los Rios. The houses there weren't built up on pilings, so they had no underneath like many other Canal Zone houses. Instead, each one had a paved driveway with a cement walkway through a diminutive front yard to the front door.

A table in Tom's yard supported a stereo powered by a chain of extension cords running inside the house. The music was loud, beer was flowing and people were dancing. The crowd spilled across the yard, over the driveway and out onto the road.

Bobby parked in the middle of the action, and Carol and I sat on the opened tailgate. Other party-goers glad of a chance to sit joined us. A tanned, boyish-looking guy I didn't know plopped down beside me, careful not to spill his Balboa Beer.

"I don't think I know you," he said, as he lit a cigarette. "Want one?"

"Don't smoke," I said and shrugged.

"I'm Craig," he said, giving me a long slow nod, looking all around me to see what I was drinking. "Not a drinker either?"

"Nope."

"Not many like you down here.

"I guess I'm a one-of-a-kind type of person."

From the glow of the house lights, I saw that Craig's

hair was thick, brown and wavy, like mine. His skin, also like mine, was the same tan color of someone who had lived in the Canal Zone for years.

His eyes, on the other hand, weren't at all like my dark-brown ones. They were unexpectedly blue, the bluest eyes I'd ever seen. His startling eye color was heightened by the blue-striped button-down shirt tucked neatly into his jeans to show off his oversized Panama Canal Zone belt buckle.

"So, *señorita* one-of-a-kind type of person, do you have a name?"

"Judy. Judy Armbruster."

"Armbruster?" He hesitated. "You wouldn't happen to be Ed Armbruster's daughter?"

His earnest look amused me. "That's my dad," I said, trying to sound carefree and reckless, to match his cocky self-confidence.

"Well, then, I do know you. We're not strangers after all."

"Okay, if you say so." I sneaked a quick look to Carol behind me, rolling my eyes. She smiled and shrugged, as if to say, "I don't know what to make of him."

"Seriously," Craig went on. "My dad flies the Cessna out of Gamboa. I've probably seen you at the airfield a half-dozen times. You were younger then, not nearly as cute."

"Maybe," I said, feigning a lack of interest. "I don't know."

Craig wasn't at all reluctant to talk about himself. His parents, both teachers in the Canal Zone schools, had lived in Gamboa, too, for a short time on the Ridge. Then they got a house in Los Rios where they'd been living now for several years. Craig had graduated from Balboa High a couple of years before, then attended college in California for a year.

"I'm home now to go to Canal Zone Junior College for another year. I really missed being here," he said, and took a long swallow of beer. "Living here gets in your blood."

We bantered and chatted. We danced to my favorite Beatles song, *Something in the Way She Moved*. Time seemed to fly by, and I was surprised when close to eleven o'clock, Tom's mother came out. The party was over. She was tired and we were keeping her up.

Bobby climbed into his pickup and hollered out to the crowd. "Who's ready to go home?"

"Not me!" a loud chorus shouted back.

"I'm headed to the Causeway," Bobby called out to the crowd, and in no time at all passengers filled the back of the truck and more took over the front seat, so Carol and I stayed in the back. So did Craig.

By the time we arrived at the gravel patch at the end of the Causeway, other cars were already parked in a circle. Bobby and the convoy of cars following him joined them as passengers crawled out to gather for shoulder-to-shoulder drinking and mindless chatter. Some of the crowd stood over by the rocks or the tree line, while others leaned on the cars.

I walked with Craig to the shore, where water lapped against the rocks, ebbing and flowing. Across the inlet, the lights of Panama City flickered and their silvery reflections danced on the dark bay. Queen's *Bohemian Rhapsody* filtered out of some car speakers behind us.

"Turn it up!" someone called.

Craig chucked pebbles in the water, making tiny splashes. Pensive, he shuffled his feet in the gravel. Searching for something to say, I told him about my friend, Mark, whose car had gone into the bay close to where we stood.

"How'd that happen?"

"Apparently Mark and his girlfriend drove out here at high tide. When he was turning around, the gas pedal stuck, and he drove his car right in."

"Were they all right?"

"Yeah, good thing both windows were down, so they could squeeze out."

There was still more to tell and Craig wanted to hear it.

"Well, you know, the Pacific Ocean is higher than the Atlantic. Tides on the Pacific Side can recede twelve feet or more. So the next day, when the tide went far out, the car sat there in the mushy sand."

"What happened then?"

"Mark's dad called his friends in the four-wheeler club, who brought Jeeps and winches. They hooked up the car and yanked it out. Of course they loved the challenge, but for Mark and his girlfriend, it was truly a close call. Imagine, if their car windows had been up—they probably would have drowned."

Craig shook his head. "That must have happened when I was in the States. I don't remember hearing about it."

"Yeah, well, now it's just another story to pass around on the Causeway."

An hour or so later, people began leaving and Bobby's truck had more riders leaving with us than had ridden in. It was always that way. Someone would catch a ride out here and not have a way home, but there was always a car going back. You might have to ride on a hood or in a trunk, but you could at least get back to the Yacht Club and find another ride going your way from there. Carol, Craig, and I all piled in with the rest.

As usual, an MP stood guard at the security entrance to Fort Amador, but there was no MP at the exit when Bobby pulled off beside the bus stop shelter near my house. After midnight on Saturday nights, MPs were used to Zonian kids leaving the Yacht Club and the Causeway, so they ignored us. To get out of the truck bed, Carol and I had to struggle over other passengers' legs, and when my feet hit the pavement, I turned back to look at Craig.

"I'll call you," he said.

We waved to Bobby as he drove off heading to Balboa. A few minutes later, Carol and I were falling asleep in my bedroom, the evening's events replaying in our minds.

Judy holding a sloth near Madden Dam

43

My last year at Balboa High School was better than I could ever have imagined. I'd taken two summer-school classes for required credits, so my application for early graduation was approved. In June 1976, at the end of my eleventh-grade year, I would graduate from high school.

That first semester was a wonderful blur. Craig and I were dating, both planning to get college degrees and eventually raise our own kids in the Canal Zone—possibly together.

For the time being, we attended football games, went to late parties and worked the hot-dog stand. Whenever we had a little money, we ate at the Yacht Club, the American Legion or the Knights of Columbus, whispering and confiding in each other. With friends we went into Panama City and splurged at Napoli's, eating pizzas, talking loud, and telling stories. Other times, we pooled our funds to buy *empanadas* or wontons at the YMCA or bowling alley, laughing and holding hands.

Craig and I swam at the pool, the beach, and the Gamboa Waterhole—old favorites that suddenly seemed new. We spent long lazy afternoons talking with his friends Paul, Tom or Steve and Craig and I rarely missed an episode of *General Hospital*. If we had to miss it, someone always filled us in on the story.

Carol began dating Wilbur, occasionally double-dating with Craig and me, but not often, because Craig and

Wilbur didn't see things eye to eye. No matter. Carol and I had chorus class together, so we saw each other regularly, and most nights, we talked on the phone. If our boyfriends weren't available, we fell into our old routine of going to movies and hanging out at the Causeway or Yacht Club.

Around Christmas, Carol and I sang in the annual chorus concert at the Balboa Theater. As we stood there on the risers in our long white choir dresses, Carol told me she and Wilbur were planning to marry at the end of the school year. When she grabbed my hand and squeezed it, we both teared up, knowing it was our last Christmas concert. I'd be at college for what should have been our senior year, and she'd be married and living somewhere in the States, where she'd promised her mom she'd finish her last year of school.

Over the holidays, we both gushed over wedding magazines. Mom and Dad wanted me to attend Canal Zone Junior College for one year, but I had other plans. Accepted at three Stateside colleges, I chose Eastern Kentucky University. It was small, affordable and accredited, and since my dad's sister lived an hour away, my parents felt good about my decision. It wasn't the college they'd hoped I would choose and I wasn't even sure it was where I really wanted to go, but Craig wanted me to go to Eastern Kentucky and that made all the difference.

Living in Kentucky would be like living in a foreign country, so Craig and I went to the library to read all we could about life there. I was somewhat familiar with the area, because several times I'd visited the farm where my cousins lived outside of Lexington. Kentucky was pretty, quiet, and completely different. If nothing else, I was ready for different.

For all of its exotic and wondrous nature, life in the Canal Zone could be monotonous. The sameness of each day of every year created a desire in some Zonians, particularly young ones, for something else, for relief. The sun always came up at about 6:30 and set about 6:15. By 6:30 P.M., it was always dark and the streetlights were on.

Every day was hot and humid, with some days a little hotter and a little more humid. At the same time every day during the six-month rainy season, it rained for an hour or two and then the sun would come out, making the air steamy. An occasional errant heavy tropical storm might surprise us with much more rain and wind, but for the most part the days were all the same.

I was ready for more choices than the milk in the red, blue, or yellow carton. Not really a choice for our family. We only bought the red carton milk—the others didn't pass the taste test. If the commissary happened to be out, we'd have no cereal until the stock was replenished. I thought it was time to find out what I'd been missing and what life in the States was really like.

44

In February, a few months before my graduation, I walked into my fifth-period English class just as the bell rang. I hadn't yet taken my seat when Mr. Wall said he wanted to see me after school. His reputation for sternness was legendary, but I couldn't think of a reason why he'd want to see me. After all, I had made it into the classroom before the bell—that's what counted. I told myself to focus on English and ignore the nagging questions about what I could possibly have done wrong.

Staying after school meant I'd have to walk, as the bus would already have left. I'd walked home many times, though its different walking home when I wanted to, versus not knowing why my English teacher wanted to see me after school.

All during class I kept groping for some inkling of why Mr. Wall wanted to see me. No ideas came. He kept on talking about nouns, verbs, pronouns and sentence structure, as if it was the most important topic in the world. When I realized I'd lost my place on my assignment, I tried frantically to focus my attention. *Please, Mr. Wall, don't call on me.*

I glanced over at Theresa for a hint to get me back on track. She saw me, but couldn't help. If Mr. Wall had asked to see me after class, clearly I was trouble and she wanted no part of that. He did not tolerate nonsense. Thankfully, I found my place in the book and concentrated.

When the last bell rang, I stowed my books in my locker

and walked back to Mr. Wall's third-floor classroom. He sat behind his desk, head bent over a stack of papers, and I hesitated to interrupt his reading. I'd have liked to turn around and hurry to my bus.

"Hi," I said after a moment.

He lifted his head, fixed his eyes on mine, and said without any preamble, "What do you know about what's going on in Panama?"

His question caught me off guard. What did the affairs in Panama have to do with anything at school? Needing something to say, I launched into an account of what had happened a few days before when Craig and I had tried to go shopping on *Avenida Central.* I'd wanted to go to the Oriental stores for some incense and a new burner and maybe pick up some earrings from a street vendor—nothing special. Craig had parked in a Canal Zone parking lot and we were about to walk across Fourth of July Avenue to the Panama Side when a CZ police officer waved us over.

"It's best to stay out of the city for a few days," he told us. "There's trouble." So naturally, we left.

Similar things had happened before. Every once in a while, protests and demonstrations made going into the city unsafe, though lately it seemed to be happening more often. There were times when SCN aired a public-service announcement suggesting that Americans stay within the borders of the Canal Zone for maximum safety.

I told Dad I found those announcements amusing, since there were no identifiable borders between the Canal Zone and Panama. The only fences, security posts, or checkpoints were at military bases. Going from Panama to the Canal Zone or vice versa was easy. You just walked across the street. Every day, Panamanians crossed the street into the Canal Zone and Americans crossed the street into Panama.

"Well then, in times of trouble," Dad said, "don't cross the street."

Mr. Wall pressed on. "What do you know about the on-going Panama Canal treaty negotiations?"

"I…uh…nothing," I confessed.

When Mr. Wall gave me his famous hard stare, the type that liquefies your insides, I had to look away to stare at the tree outside the window. Rumor had it that he'd once thrown a boy out that window, instead of doing what a normal teacher would and send him to the principal. I shifted my gaze to my leather sandals and painted toenails.

"Ah …" he finally said. "Do you pay attention to the news?"

"I'm usually doing homework or reading a book." No way was I going to answer that question honestly. I certainly wouldn't tell him I only watched *General Hospital* and occasionally *Perry Mason*. I figured the reading a book answer was safe, for after all, he did teach English.

"I see." He nodded, then went on to explain that General Torrijos and the U.S. State Department were negotiating a new treaty that would greatly affect Zonian families. It was possible that we might even lose the Canal Zone.

"The results of this treaty will affect you and your life," he told me. "Would you be willing to help hand out flyers tomorrow after school to announce an upcoming rally?"

I didn't know why Mr. Wall had chosen me to hand out the flyers, but I was genuinely pleased. That was when my world became different, when a certain sense of innocence slipped away. I began to pay attention to the news, listen to talk around town, and ask questions.

The next day after school, Craig and I went over to the commissary. As people walked out with their groceries, we handed them flyers. We met others in the parking lot and left them flyers, too. Then we crossed over Stevens Circle and handed out flyers to Zonians collecting their mail at the post office. To all who would listen, we stressed the urgency of attending the upcoming rally and when we were done, we went to the clubhouse and ordered french fries.

"What do you think this all means?" I asked Craig, squirting *Maggie* ketchup onto the paper plate.

"I don't know," he said. "I did hear some talk at the college today."

"Like what?"

"Well, maybe a sickout is going to happen."

"What's that?"

Craig gave me his best explanation. Since workers in the Canal Zone were employees of the U.S. government, it was illegal for them to strike, but workers wanted some say in the treaty negotiations. After all, their lives and families would be affected.

"Why should diplomats determine labor matters," Craig said, "without consulting the very people who perform the labors? America works by considering the majority opinion."

I agreed that's what we'd been taught.

"See, apparently, the U.S. Assistant Secretary of the Army has a different view," Craig told me, "freezing some wages and making cutbacks. When the Canal Zone governor told him this might not go over well with Panama Canal employees, the secretary told him not to worry because Canal workers were all 'gutless sheep.'"

I was stunned. "He said that?"

Craig shrugged. "That's what I heard."

Gutless sheep? What an insult! I wondered then if Dad would go to the rally.

Life in the Canal Zone centered on the Canal, naturally. More than once, we children had been taken on field trips to the Miraflores Locks for a firsthand appreciation of the wonder of American ingenuity and the hard work and sacrifice of previous generations of workers. In the visitors' tower, we'd stood at the large plate glass windows watching workers throw and tie cables from the ships to the locomotives called "mules" that pulled the vessels through each chamber.

All of us who lived in the Canal Zone were connected either directly or indirectly with the work of the Canal. Putting a ship through the Canal was a team effort, so if you weren't a member of one of the teams that helped to run the Canal, you were supporting team members.

Teachers were there to educate the children of the Canal Zone employees. Doctors and dentists were there to treat those who worked on the Canal and their families. Bus drivers, cafeteria workers, and commissary managers served Panama Canal employees. The military was there to protect U.S. interests in Panama, as well as in the Southern Hemisphere.

A community with a purpose, the Canal Zone was unified in maintaining and operating the Canal. We took pride in our important contribution to the world at large. We also knew that without the Canal, we wouldn't be here.

I knew Dad wouldn't sit on the sidelines. Not Dad. Not me, either. No way.

45

The next Sunday after church, I was in our kitchen squeezing limes to make limeade, a chore I hated. Lime juice always found the one cut on my finger, hot and stinging.

Dad walked in and took a frying pan from the oven's bottom drawer. "Don't use a lot of sugar," he commented, seeing what I was about.

"Uh-huh," I answered absentmindedly as I scooped in my usual amount.

I liked my limeade sweeter than Dad did.

Dad was browning hamburger meat, and it sizzled. Probably making spaghetti for supper.

He spoke to my back, as I washed the juice press.

"Go tell your sisters to stay off the phone. I have a call in for your grandma. No one is to use the phone until my call comes through."

Putting in a Stateside call was a process. First, it required someone going to the telephone office, reserving and paying for the phone call. On Mother's Day and other major holidays, the line was quite long and it was hard to get on the schedule. Once the call was reserved and paid for, at your appointed time, the switchboard operator placed the call to the States. Then the line was transferred to your house. At the cost of two dollars a minute, we didn't make many long-distance phone calls.

Shortly after dinner, our phone rang. I picked it up and said "Armbruster's residence," the way Dad wanted us to

answer the phone, though when he wasn't around I'd simply say, "Hello." If I knew it was Kim or Carol calling, I'd
say, "Aaaaloo," like the Panamanians. I'd gotten so good at
that, you wouldn't know I was American. Tonight though,
I answered the phone Dad's way.

"I have a call to Margaret Armbruster in New Port
Richey, Florida, for Edwin Armbruster," the operator said
in her crisp business-like tone.

"Thank you," Dad's voice broke in from his bedroom
extension. "Judy, you can get off the phone now."

Too late. Grandma now knew I was on the phone.

"Judy, you on the phone?" Her familiar voice chirped
over the line.

"Hi, Grandma."

"Hi, yourself. How's school?" I could hear Harry chattering in the background.

"Fine. What have you …"

"Judy," Dad interrupted, "I need to talk to Grandma."

"Nice talking to you, Grandma. Oh, yeah, bye, Dad." I
hung up quickly.

I motioned to Debi and we crept over to our parents'
closed bedroom door. The walls were paper-thin, so we
clearly heard Dad's side of the conversation. I don't know
why he bothered to shut the door. Our parents had long ago
learned that if they wanted to discuss things privately, they
had to sit in the car to talk or wait until we were asleep.

"Watch the news the next few days or so," Dad said to
Grandma. "Might not be on tomorrow night's news, but
keep watching. Also, could you pick up the *Tampa Tribune*
or *St. Pete Times* to see if we made it in those newspapers?
I get the *Miami Herald* here, but I'm curious if other papers are covering it."

Silence. Grandma must be talking.

"… A little trouble," continued Dad. "We'll be fine."

Silence again. Debi and I exchanged a questioning look.

Dad said goodbye and hung up just as Debi and I scrambled into Connie's room, which was closest. We grabbed a couple of teen magazines and flopped on the bed, but Dad walked by without noticing us. Then we heard his footsteps in the living room, the front door close, and then the car leave the driveway.

"Told you, Debi," I said. "Something's going on."

"What d'you think it means?"

"I don't know. You know what Craig said and I told Margie about it. I wanted to know if she'd heard the same thing in her classes at the college."

"Well?"

"She said it's complicated, that I wouldn't understand."

I buried my resentment. Margie still treated me like an annoying background presence. When I'd asked her about going to Canal Zone College, she'd said, "Why don't you ask Craig?" When I'd asked her about her boyfriend, she'd mumbled a few words, then walked away. Our conversations were on the level of "Pass the salt and don't forget it's your turn to wash the dishes." Talking to Margie about what was happening in the Canal Zone would get me nowhere.

At school on Monday morning, there was plenty of excited but uncertain talk about a sickout. American workers were already calling in sick.

On Tuesday, more workers called in sick. When the bus pulled up at the high school, it was turned away. Too many teachers had called in sick and there weren't enough substitutes. Any available substitutes had been sent to the elementary schools.

On Wednesday, school was cancelled again, except for the two elementary schools that had enough teachers. The rest of the Canal Zone schools were closed. A few more American workers were sick.

Thursday, with school cancelled again, Craig and I

headed to the bowling alley to crowd around a table with fellow juniors and seniors. Paul took up a collection for two plates of french fries and an order of wontons. Then Craig pulled out a copy of the *Miami Herald* and read us the report. "Last Monday, more than 700 of the 3,500 American Panama Canal workers called in sick. Today the number was close to 2,000. Over a hundred ships were lined up in the outer area of the Canal, waiting for pilots to transit the ships. Unfortunately, many of the Canal pilots were 'out sick.'"

A weird quiet settled over our normally boisterous group. In less than a week, the Panama Canal had effectively shut down. We had proven that we were not "gutless sheep."

Someone at the table remarked it was like that small band of Americans who had defended the Alamo. Then someone else countered that all the defenders of the Alamo had been killed.

With that, Craig and I left and drove down the Causeway to see the unusual sight of so many ships waiting to enter the Canal.

That evening Grandma called to tell us the Canal Zone situation was making both the early and late national news. She promised to send clippings from the *Tribune* and *Times* right away. I read the local and stateside newspapers voraciously. I questioned Dad, Mom, Craig's parents and my teachers. I listened to people talking at the post office, the bowling alley and the commissary. I was hungry for information and trying to make sense of a world that had been so orderly, but now was in limbo.

Most Zonians agreed that a new treaty with Panama was necessary, for certain elements of the old treaty were outdated and no longer appropriate for the times in which we lived. What Zonians opposed, unanimously, was the secrecy of the negotiations between the U.S.

State Department and Panama, completely ignoring those Americans who lived, operated and knew the workings of the Canal. We also opposed the U.S .State Department's obvious contempt for Americans who lived in the Canal Zone. We resented being treated like naïve, petulant children in a political game.

When asked about the treaty, American Canal Zone Governor Parfitt stated, "The morale problem will continue until the treaty provisions are on the table and known."

Despite what the Stateside papers wrote, the Canal Zone was neither a colony nor a territory of the United States. It was a zone of land that the U.S. controlled inside a foreign country. Individual citizens couldn't own private property there, because the whole Canal Zone was U.S. government property.

We Canal Zone residents regarded our host country of Panama as a welcome part of our lives. We bought in their fish markets, ate in their restaurants, danced in their clubs, shopped in their stores and reveled at their carnivals. Some Zonians owned property in the country of Panama, while others were members of Panamanian civic organizations.

We respected the Panamanians, though we distrusted the tyrannical government headed by General Torrijos and with good reason. The intimate knowledge Canal Zonians had of the Panamanian leader would have stunned the State Department, had they asked us, which they didn't. The State Department had no interest in hearing what Zonians had to say. To them, those of us who lived in the Canal Zone were rogue Americans who were ignorant of how the world really works.

We Canal Zone sons and daughters were taken aback by the rancor of Stateside Americans. It had been our belief that Americans worked together to resolve issues. We thought Americans defended each other. After years of watching World War II movies and local news on SCN headlining the ceremonies for incoming and departing military officers, we had believed that Americans were united. For us, that's what made America so special.

The sickout pierced the protected simplicity of my Canal Zone world. I was learning that there were Americans who actively worked against other Americans and would use unscrupulous means to justify their own ends.

By Friday, Day Five of the sickout, 140 ships were lined up outside the entrance to the Canal and ship owners were losing millions. The Canal was practically paralyzed, with motionless ships anchored as far as ten miles out on both the Atlantic and Pacific Sides. In Washington, the Secretary of the Army said he was ordering soldiers into the Zone, because the sickout was disrupting international trade.

On Saturday afternoon, Governor Parfitt made some concessions and the Panama Canal ship pilots and tugboat operators went back to work transiting the vessels immediately. There would be no reprisals for workers who had called in sick. Still, a new unease permeated our tropical breezes.

Two months later, in the midst of Canal Zone uncertainty, I graduated from Balboa High School. I was sixteen.

46

I spent my seventeenth birthday gazing out my dorm window at Eastern Kentucky University. Maples, dogwood, and sycamores were beginning to glow with their bold yellows, oranges, and reds. Some trees already had shed leaves onto the browning grass. My excitement over this spectacular show of nature was one more thing that my roommates found odd about me. After six weeks, I still felt out of place.

From Mom's 500-page book, recording her genealogical line from the time America was still a British colony, I had learned that I'm descended from an American Revolutionary soldier, that my grandfather had fought in World War II and that my own father was in the U.S. Air Force when the Vietnam War began. Even so, I was a stranger in my own country.

Letters came from home. There had been several car bombs and bomb scares throughout the Canal Zone. Debi wrote that one car bomb had actually exploded in the parking lot at the Commissary and shaken the entire Balboa gym. Mom wrote about policemen at every corner and an increased number of MPs at the military-post checkpoints. Cars were randomly searched and Zonians no longer had free access to military bases. Sometimes Mom included newspaper clippings in her letters.

It was October 6, 1976, and with earphones and a small transistor radio, I lay on my dorm bed listening to an NPR station. It was a month before the presidential election

Judy starting college Eastern Kentucky University

and Gerald Ford and Jimmy Carter were in a debate at San Francisco's Palace of Fine Arts Theater. It began at 6:30 P.M. Pacific time, while in eastern Kentucky it was 9:30.

My two roommates were on their own beds, studying quietly. Anxiously, I listened through long tedious answers about Russia, Rhodesia, and the Middle East. When the moderator said there were just twelve minutes left for the debate, my heart raced. Was that enough time to ask the quintessential question for thousands of Americans—the fate of the Canal Zone?

At last it came. The first question went to Governor Carter. I smiled to myself when I heard Mr. Trewhitt of the *Baltimore Sun* say that the largest volume of communication he'd received for this debate concerned Panama. Well, of course. Was there any question more important? I held my breath.

"Would you, as president, be prepared to sign a treaty that at a fixed date would yield administrative and economic control of the Canal Zone?"

Motionless, I listened with every fiber of my body as

Mr. Carter ranted against President Ford. Then, in a deliberate and clear tone, Carter said, "I would never give up complete control or practical control of the Panama Canal Zone. I would continue to negotiate with the Panamanians."

I let out a breath. Then, in case he might be misunderstood, Carter reiterated: "I might be willing to reduce to some degree the military emplacements in the Panama Canal Zone, but I would not relinquish control of the Panama Canal Zone any time in the foreseeable future." President Ford agreed. He wouldn't relinquish control either.

So intense was my concentration that I didn't realize my roommates had already turned off their lights and fallen asleep. Just as well. Now I could savor this delicious radiant surety.

I turned off my own bedside light and closed my eyes. My dreams would come true after all. Oh, there might be a little bit of trouble, but we'd been there before. No matter who became president, both candidates had emphatically declared that the United States would not give up the Canal Zone. My world was safe. I fell asleep, remembering the night smells and sounds of home.

On November 2, 1976, Jimmy Carter was elected president of the United States. By Thanksgiving, I had pledged to a sorority. With that honor came the privilege of moving to Walters Hall to live on a designated floor with my new sorority sisters and my sister pledge, Kelly, invited me to her Ohio home for the long holiday weekend. Thanksgiving Day was filled with food, Kelly's relatives and football games on television. I couldn't recall ever watching TV on a Thanksgiving Day. My own family would be spending that day with several other Canal Zone families, preparing a large dinner, telling stories and playing board games. The next day, Friday, when Kelly's family got up at five A.M. to go shopping, my friends at home would be headed to the beach.

Saturday night, Kelly and I went to a party at her friend's house, where one of the guests led us to a basement furnished as a family den. Several well-padded chairs and a plaid couch faced a television and bookcases filled with knickknacks. Chips and cookies sat on a card table. Bottles of soda were crammed into an ice-chest on the floor. In the corner, a stereo played the newest Stevie Wonder album. The lights were low, and a few couples had found their own intimate spaces. Left on my own after some brief introductions, I sat on a footstool by the stereo pretending to be entirely engrossed in reading an album cover, wanting to be anywhere but here.

A tall, lanky, red-haired boy looked straight at me. "Want to make out?"

"I don't even know you." I returned my attention to the album cover.

"That's okay. That's how we get to know each other."

"I'll probably never even see you again. I'm not from here."

"That's okay, too. Sometimes it works better that way."

What worked better that way? Kissing some boy you've never seen, just to pass time? Nope. I wasn't the least bit interested.

Kelly was on the couch, cuddled in some guy's arms. The next evening, she'd be cuddled with her college boyfriend in the dorm's public TV lounge.

I picked up a Steve Miller Band album and began reading the blurbs on the back. The redhead walked away to find another make-out partner. Feeling miserable, I hoped Kelly would remember she'd promised her mom we'd be back before ten P.M. to pack. We were to leave early the next morning. To my relief, she did remember, and we left on time.

When we got back to campus, I was amazed to find Craig sitting in the public lounge of my dorm. I was even more surprised when he told me he was there to stay.

"I know," he said, "we agreed to live in separate states for at least a year, but things changed."

Our plan had been to live in separate states to allow us to see where we wanted our relationship to go. We'd both thought the plan was smart and grown-up. I hadn't expected him to move here to Richmond, Kentucky.

"Uh, well, you can't stay here," I said. "This is an all-girls dorm. You'd be noticed," I teased. "Where are you staying right now?"

He was staying at a hotel. The next day we found him a studio apartment in a grand historic hotel in downtown Richmond. A few days later, he found a job. Later, he applied to attend EKU for the spring semester.

Craig and I spent every minute together that I wasn't in class and he wasn't working. It *was* nice to have someone who already knew me and that I could be myself with. I was tired of being a square peg.

In December, I saw my first snowfall. Tiny white flecks swirled in front of me as I walked to class. Hard to believe, but I didn't make the connection at first. It wasn't until someone exclaimed, "It's snowing!" that I noticed the flakes. By the next morning, the campus was white with snow, so three of my sorority sisters helped me build a snowman. Then later, Craig and I had a snow fight. By nightfall, I was ready for summer and hot sunny days.

When I pulled out the stylish coat Mom and I had bought for me in Florida, I found that it didn't repel the wet snow and wasn't even warm. My new knee-high boots weren't waterproof either and their slick soles made walking almost impossible. Mom and I had been duped by the Florida saleswoman's promise this was a perfect outfit for winter.

"I'm downright freezing," I told Craig one day after class.

He smiled. "I know what you mean. It takes time to get used to winter weather."

"Why don't you wear more clothes?" Kelly asked one day after I walked in from class to attend a pledge meeting. I had taken off my coat, revealing a thin sweater underneath.

"You should wear a t-shirt under your sweater, maybe even a thicker sweater."

The next day I did as Kelly suggested, only to find that then my fancy coat wouldn't button and thicker socks made my boots uncomfortably tight. The slippery sidewalks were enough of a challenge and worse, I couldn't breathe wearing so many clothes. After my first class, I hurried back to the dorm and took some of them off, aware that it was going to be a long winter. Fortunately I'd be going home to Panama for Christmas.

During Christmas break, Craig stayed in Kentucky to work. I couldn't wait to get home. Three luscious weeks of lounging in the pools, at the beaches, in the warmth! Hours of blissful conversation with Debi and heavy involvement with Margie's wedding in the chapel at Fort Amador made the days fly by much too fast. I did not miss Kentucky at all.

The trouble in Panama had subsided, and Canal Zone life had resumed its usual pace. Although Panama's leader, General Torrijos, hadn't accepted President Carter's announcement that Americans had no intention of leaving, most Zonians had confidence in the new American president's promise.

Dad warned us though that things would never be the same. "There's a different type of tension here," he said. I boarded the plane for the United States wondering how things would be when I returned home for the summer.

In Lexington, Kentucky, my plane landed during a heavy winter storm. Craig picked me up at the airport, excited to hear about my trip home. Over the holidays, my mom had suggested I try to get a part-time job and Craig agreed. "Trouble is," he said, "it's hard to find one in Richmond."

I asked a few sorority sisters how to find a job on campus. No one knew. "*We* do *not* have to work," my pledge mother said. "Our work is service to the college and community." Completely missing her innuendo, I wasn't concerned when she wrote something in her notebook.

Undaunted, I bought a newspaper and studied the scant classifieds. By the next day, I had a job waitressing at the Union 76 Truck Stop, a few miles up I-75. Craig was willing to drive me to work for my 3-11 shift. It was my first real job and I found it rewarding. For the next few days I proudly wore my blue polyester pantsuit uniform in the dorm, but whispers and sidelong looks soon let me know my sorority sisters didn't share my enthusiasm for my employment. I began using the back door closer to my dorm room. If I had to choose between the sorority and my job, I wasn't sure the sorority would win. Mom was right; I loved the feeling of having my own money.

47

For my class, "Man, Culture, and Society," I was told to bring in a current-event piece every week. My silver-haired professor wanted us to summarize an article and voice our opinion. He said it would make the class more personally relevant for us. I agreed.

My first story was a clipping from the *Star and Herald* that Mom had sent me from Panama. The Panamanian dictator, General Torrijos, had revealed that he was pleased Jimmy Carter had won the election because, he said, Carter had a great sense of American shame and therefore Panama would get a much better treaty than otherwise. I was confused. The Americans I knew back home felt no shame about the work we did in the Canal Zone. On the contrary, all of us were proud of our contributions toward helping Panama to do well, along with the Panama Canal's service to the world at large.

So I asked the class, "What shame do Americans have about the Panama Canal?"

No one responded. I wanted my classmates and my professor to agree with me that we had nothing to be ashamed for. I wanted them to be interested in my favorite topic. In the uncomfortable silence, I realized that my classmates didn't know anything about the Panama Canal or even much about America's influence in the world.

Beyond that, I was stunned when my professor said I would have done better to choose an article from an American newspaper. The *Star and Herald* was an

American newspaper, its reputation equal to any other American papers. Still, I didn't want to be considered a troublemaker. I could easily find articles on my chosen subject using sources more acceptable to the professor. I was not about to give up.

The next article I used from the *New York Times* sharply criticized America for *stealing* the Panama Canal. The author dared to write that American history books conveniently omitted incriminating evidence of America's theft. Basing my remarks on that piece, I argued to my classmates and the professor that we couldn't steal something that hadn't existed in the first place. Before the Americans came, there was no canal and no canal locks. There was only jungle, malaria, yellow fever, and the failed attempt by France to build a canal.

I explained that because Americans had helped Panama win the land from Colombia, maybe the land needed to be returned to Colombia. Finally, I contended that the author of the article who claimed that Americans sat in colonial luxury in the Canal Zone surely had never been to the same Canal Zone where I lived.

When I sat down, the professor pointed out that there were other current events that might interest me as well. I couldn't think of a single one.

In my free time, I sat with Craig on the stairs of the Powell Student Union watching a small contingent of Black Panthers marching under the covered veranda. Dressed in tight black pants, black jackets, and black berets, their precise disciplined steps affirmed their passion. I recognized one of them from my class, but he had never spoken to me, as stern and focused in class as in his marching.

One day I asked Craig, "Why do you think they march like that every afternoon?"

My fascination irritated Craig. "Black Power," he said.

"Doesn't it remind you of the Panama National Guard?"

The Panama National Guard, also spit-and-polish perfect, was commanded by Panamanian dictator, General Torrijos—the same Torrijos whose opponents had been imprisoned, exiled or found mysteriously dead. The same Torrijos, who had led the push to renegotiate the Panama Canal treaty. The same dictator, who was more than delighted that our new American president could be manipulated by a strong sense of misplaced guilt.

Craig understood for he, too, worried about the situation in the Canal Zone. How would the proposed Panama Treaties affect the future of Americans living there? How would it affect *our* planned future?

I let activities with my sorority decline, a missed fraternity-sorority mixer here, a mixed social there. Eventually, I stopped receiving invitations for sorority events. I think the final straw was when several seniors from my sorority noticed me in my waitress uniform getting into a 10-year-old faded blue Impala driven by the black cook from the Union 76 Truck Stop. Had Murray been born in different circumstances, he might have been a linebacker for his high-school football team. As it was, he was a kind middle-aged man with three children and a wife who tried, in vain, to bleach the grease stains out of his white t-shirts. Since Craig's work hours had changed to night shifts I was grateful for the ride to work. My sorority never officially removed my name from their invite list. My invitations simply "got lost in the campus mail."

If I had thought I'd make friends with other waitresses at my job, I was mistaken there, too. I had nothing in common with them either. They worked hard to provide for their families and had never been more than twenty miles from their homes. My talk about Panama, travel, school events and, of course, Craig, only isolated me. I counted the days to the semester's end.

Mom wrote, "What are your plans for the summer?

Connie will be a cheerleader for the Balboa Rams this summer and Debi will be playing softball. We're coming to the States the first of August. Maybe you want to find a roommate and stay at your job to save money for the fall semester? It would sure help us out if you could pay for some of your books."

My eyes smarted and I sighed heavily. I knew I couldn't get a summer job in the Canal Zone, so going home wouldn't happen. But one thing I knew for sure—Richmond, Kentucky, was not a good fit for me. This was not where I belonged.

Craig planned to move in with a friend in a rented trailer at the end of town. He increased his work hours and scheduled his classes for the fall. He encouraged me to look for a new job in town and talked about spending any free time with me at the lake or going to the movies. Reluctantly, I scheduled my fall classes but couldn't bring myself to check the bulletin boards for a summer roommate.

Then I saw a flyer in the hallway and knew I had my answer—at least for the moment. I enrolled in a summer program in Guadalajara, Mexico.

48

Dad arranged for a retired military friend from the Canal Zone, Colonel Smith and his wife, to meet me at the airport in Tucson, Arizona, where the colonel helped me to buy traveler's checks and update my visa to Mexico. It was good to see someone I'd known back home. We talked about old times and laughed at mutual recollections.

"Young lady, how did you get an official passport?" the colonel asked while we waited in line for the visa stamp. I fingered the lettering on the small booklet, my first individual passport. Before, I'd been a member of a family passport with Mom and my sisters.

I shrugged. "One of Dad's friends at the embassy, I guess."

He laughed and explained that an official passport is only for diplomats and people traveling on state business. A different color from an ordinary passport, it isn't issued lightly.

Then it made sense to me why Dad had rushed us to an appointment at the embassy. Mom had reminded him that our passports weren't up for renewal, but he only gave a conspiratorial grin with a twinkle in his eyes and said he had a new connection. I smiled, remembering.

The next day I boarded a chartered bus with other American students who would attend the University of Arizona's summer-school program. Nogales, Arizona, sixty miles from Tucson, was our entry point into Mexico and where we would go through customs. The bus pulled over to an inspection area. There we all grabbed our bulging suitcases and set them on the metal tables. A Mexican customs agent glanced at my passport, recognized the official color and, without opening a single bag, told me I was cleared.

I picked up my luggage and reboarded the bus, careful not to look at anyone. My fellow student travelers' belongings were strewn haphazardly over the tables being examined. When they hurriedly shoved their t-shirts, jeans, and underwear back into their luggage and returned to the bus, I kept my eyes glued to my paperback book.

The next time we unloaded was at the train station, where a porter took my heavy suitcase. Whether I imagined it or not, I felt as if other students watched as I followed my bags to my reserved coach. Since I was traveling alone, Mom had insisted on paying a few extra dollars for me to have a private first-class compartment. It might sound luxurious, but it was tiny, only as wide as the two-person bench seat anchored wall to wall. Six inches from my knees was a single seat with a cushion, which hid a toilet underneath. Next to that was a utility sink and above it, a narrow rectangular mirror hung by one nail. The inside walls of hospital yellow clashed with the faded maroon velour seat cushions. Black oily grime filmed the bottom half of the outside window and a sliding door with an inside latch closed off the cubicle from the corridor. At night, a Murphy bed filled the entire cabin. This would be my room for the next twenty-four hours.

The train passed through green farmland, arid desert and then the mountains and canyons of the Sierra Madre. At innumerable stops where families of track workers lived in old railway cars, ragged children rushed to the platform lugging plastic pails filled with bottled Orange Crush and Pepsi. Passengers opened their windows and reached out to exchange coins for cold drinks.

The train sped through Copper Canyon and I remembered Dad's letter suggesting I pay attention to details. After all, I'd be riding on the "American Orient Express." We went over dozens of suspension bridges and through countless dark tunnels. The train rounded mountain walls on such tight curves that at times I could look across the canyon and see the rear of the train. Soon though, the ride became excruciatingly boring.

At mealtime, I shared a table in the dining car with three other American students, two Larrys and a Gail. I translated the menu for my dinner companions and warned them about having ice in their drinks. One of the Larrys returned the favor by reporting that in 1955, a train had plunged into a canyon off this track, killing 300 people. "That was more than twenty years ago," he said, "but the tracks are just the same and the danger is still present."

His comment didn't bother me nearly as much as something the other Larry said. Apparently, in Mazatlan, a major depot where the train stopped to be reconfigured for the last leg of the trip, there were times some of the train cars had been mistakenly left behind. We were due in Mazatlan at midnight, so if I was asleep and not paying attention, I might wake up in the wrong city.

My tablemates told me they didn't have private berths to sleep in. They were in the third-class cars, called *Burro Class*, where six or more passengers crammed into row after row of bench seats with suitcases and shopping bags packed into any available space. They slept sitting up. Only those with window seats breathed fresh air. Grateful for Mom's foresight, I bid my fellow passengers good night and headed with new appreciation to my private quarters.

Nothing went wrong in Mazatlan and a school representative met us at the station in Guadalajara. He directed us to an assigned taxi, where I met my new American housemates. None of them had ever crossed a border before and were pleased to have someone along who was comfortable in a foreign country—me—at last, appreciated.

The taxi took us to our home-stay family in an upper-middle-class neighborhood. Their house reminded me of the nicer houses in Panama City. Tropical ferns, hibiscus, palms, and orchids crowded nicely in maintained green grass around a concrete patio and an ornate iron fence with a sliding gate securing the home and yard from any intruders.

Inside, spotless white glazed-tile flooring spread throughout the two-story house. My roommate, Carrie, and I shared a room with twin beds and a full bathroom. The other two American girls shared an identical room across the hall. In the master bedroom, the middle-aged homeowner, a widow, shared space with her teen-age daughter. Bedrooms for the two housemaids were downstairs.

Our second day in Mexico, I repacked my gray leather Dr. Scholl's sandals after buying a pair of soft Mexican leather huaraches at an open-air market. Mexico was good for me.

Salsa and reggae music spilled out from clusters of stores, enlivening our sunny afternoon walks to the bus stop from school. I happily boarded the garishly colored buses that clogged the busy streets. I basked in the familiar blaring sounds from honking horns and even the black smoke from tailpipes. Evenings I laughed at the high-pitched Spanish voice coming from Farrah Fawcett's lips in the dubbed version of "Charlie's Angels" and enjoyed eating delicious freshly picked tropical fruits.

Six weeks in Mexico flew by—and while I was there, I changed my school plans. Rather than return to Eastern Kentucky University, I would head to Provo, Utah, to join friends from the Canal Zone and two cousins who were attending Brigham Young University. As for Craig, I wrote to him saying that in the meantime, we would talk by phone, write letters, and meet up again in the Canal Zone during Christmas break.

When the time came for us to leave, I envied Carrie who was flying home. My return would be the mind-numbing train ride to Nogales. Our other two roommates had the *Burro* section of the train—their trip home would be even more tedious and uncomfortable than mine.

I decided it would be more fun if the three of us rode together. "You're welcome to come to my cabin, if you want," I said. They jumped at my offer. At the depot, I asked the ticket agent to exchange my private compartment for a semi-private one with two bunks.

"*Señorita*, we can no do that."

"Why not?" I handed him my official passport, slightly leaned over the counter and gave him a flirtatious smile.

"Why not, indeed," he said and called a porter to take my heavy suitcase and shopping bag crammed with a woven basket, hand-painted clay pig, carved wooden chess set and embroidered peasant shirts.

My roommates were struggling with their own luggage. "Doesn't that offend your feminist sensibilities?" they asked me. Porters were not to be found when they saw the other girls' *Clase Tercero* tickets.

I shrugged, "Not one bit. I see no reason to follow some unwritten feminist code, if it limits my opportunities. Remember, once the conductor takes your ticket, come to my *cabinero*. There's plenty of room."

My first-class coach was several cars away from the dining car and much further away from the crowded third-class bench seats.

An hour later, my two roommates and I watched Mexico pass by our window from our comfortable-by-comparison quarters. The next day, we would be back in the States.

49

My new apartment in Provo was a few blocks from Brigham Young University. I had three roommates, two from Idaho and one from Louisiana. We shared a comfortable easiness and talked a lot about our respective backgrounds. Considering my abrupt change of plans in Mexico, I'd been lucky to register in four classes. Dad's contact with another former Canal Zone friend who now worked at the university paved the way for me.

Once again I became absorbed with any news about the Panama Canal. I still intended to move back after college and eventually raise my own family there. On August 14, 1977, President Carter had made national headlines with his approval of the Panama Accord and stories about the Canal Zone and treaty negotiations abounded.

I listened to the debates on PBS, NPR, CBS, ABC, and NBC, and questioned how certain journalists could take individual facts and create such inaccurate reports against fellow Americans without being challenged. I thought it immoral and my roommates agreed.

I clung to my hopes, because the treaty hadn't yet been signed. Despite journalists' slanted reports, public-opinion polls still ran overwhelmingly against the president's signing of the treaty. Throughout my school years in the Canal Zone and even at college in Kentucky, I had been taught that our leaders in Washington were guided by the will of the people. I had believed that, but now I wasn't so sure.

Then on August 16, two days after President Carter's troubling headline news, Elvis Presley died. That night, CBS was taken to task for leading its broadcast with a lengthy segment on the Panama Canal and relegating Presley's death to a lesser spot, while other networks were applauded for their lengthy discussions of the passing of the King of Rock. I was disappointed that stories of a celebrated entertainer would overshadow the very important Panama Canal story. Sure, the news of Presley's death was noteworthy and upsetting, but couldn't the two events share equal time on television news? Surely the Canal was of greater international significance than an American rock-and-roller's demise.

Then on September 7, in a complete reversal of the promise he'd made eleven months before, President Carter signed the treaty relinquishing total control to Panama the Canal and Canal Zone. I was devastated and dumbfounded. I found it inconceivable that a United States president would lie to his people. I'd known of leaders in foreign countries who lied, stole, and cheated, but I was naïve enough to imagine that all our presidents held the same convictions as the George Washington I'd learned about in history.

As a further shock, this treaty also authorized the immediate abolishment of the Canal Zone—my home. With that, my world stopped. Where would I go from here? What was I supposed to do now? In a few weeks, I would turn eighteen.

Mom's birthday card to me contained a check and a letter, along with an account of the confusion and anger of our fellow Zonians. Groups were already writing letters to U.S. representatives and senators and asking relatives in the States to join the letter-writing campaign.

Now that I was old enough to vote, why not get involved? I sat down with my roommates and we wrote our own letters. I persuaded other classmates to do the same, though many had no idea where the Canal Zone was.

In actuality there were two treaties: one to assure the neutrality of the Panama Canal and the other to relinquish control and turn over American assets in Panama. Like thousands of other Americans, I hoped the Senate wouldn't ratify those treaties and that new negotiations would be required. I still found it inconceivable. Not only had President Carter signed away the Canal and the locks, he had signed away the Panama Canal Company infrastructure created by Americans for American interests in the Canal Zone.

At the very least, I protested to my roommates and all who would listen, our country's leaders needed to scrutinize the details of these treaties. If Jimmy Carter would blatantly lie for votes, what confidence could Canal Zone workers have that our president would protect the country's vested interests in the company for which many had worked their entire lives? U.S. citizens living abroad had families depending on them, I reminded my friends. They were not statistics on some unread government report.

I'm not sure what I expected that December when I went home for my last Christmas in the Canal Zone. On the surface, everything seemed the same. Mom and I went to the Balboa Theater and watched the high-school Christmas concert. I went to a few parties with Carol and visited other friends.

But like the insidious Panamanian humidity that seeps through your skin and leaves you exhausted, so did the realization that the Canal Zone's future was over. In a year and half, according to the recently signed treaty, the Canal Zone would cease to be. President Carter had admonished Americans that our government's focus would be a smooth transfer of the Panama Canal and its entire U.S. holdings to Panamanians. What about the Zonians?

He left them—us—hanging. Futures unknown, lives shattered.

How could anyone trust our country's president when by a pen stroke he had betrayed the American spirit that built the Panama Canal? How could U.S. journalists, supposedly schooled in objectivity, depict hard-working fellow Americans as rogue colonialists living pampered lives on some other country's land? The very idea infuriated me. No one was listening to these American citizens who lived in rented temporary government quarters. They had no chance of getting the true story out when powerful media giants portrayed Canal Zone residents as bullying the Panamanians, whom we loved.

Where does one go when the place called home will no longer exist, except as a few paragraphs in an encyclopedia? Some of my Zonian friends joined the military, some aimlessly drifted into drugs or dead-end jobs, and some went back to college to try to rebuild their shattered futures. Still others stayed in the Canal Zone, living on borrowed time until the last possible moment. I held onto my Canal Zone life by marrying Craig, for after all, he was my best friend and connection to the world I loved.

Canal Zone stamp and postmark (Letter from home)

50

I n order for the Panama Canal Treaties to become valid, two-thirds of the members of the U.S. Senate had to vote to ratify them. Debate to win the necessary sixty-seven votes began on February 7, 1978. For the first time, debate on the Senate floor would be broadcast by NPR. The fact that every American would now be able to hear the discussion in real time and know where every senator stood made some of them more than a little nervous.

Ronald Reagan, then California's former governor, led a fight against ratifying the treaties and, at times, it looked like they wouldn't pass. Opposition in the Senate was intense. During breaks of the hearing, the NPR reporter filled in with background and historical information on the Canal Zone, some accurate, some completely false. I gained new hope, however, from reports of letters flooding the Congressional mailroom, with over 70 percent of the nation against the treaties.

NPR also reported rumors of heated discussions and back-room deals between President Carter and the senators, stating that Jimmy Carter badly wanted the treaties to pass, because he was quickly losing credibility as president.

On April 18, 1978, after the longest debate in Senate history, the treaties narrowly passed. Sixty-eight senators had voted for ratification—a one-vote margin. I found it extremely disturbing to hear of United States senators saying they voted to approve these treaties, even though their constituents opposed them. Never far from my thoughts

A special insert of the local newspaper regarding new changes for Americans because of the treaties.

was the image of *candidate* Jimmy Carter promising the nation that, should he be elected president, he would never relinquish U.S. control of the Panama Canal.

In November that same year, *Playboy* published an interview with Geraldo Rivera in which he boldly expressed his slanted views on the Canal Zone controversy.

People with an agenda can spin their words to hide truth, as Rivera didn't hesitate to make clear. With pride, he recounted how he and reporters from the *Times* and the *Post* had been having dinner together and realized what power they had to manipulate the situation. He went on to admit, they were deliberately careful about what they reported, so they would not to lose *their* objective—convincing the Senate to ratify the treaties. To these reporters, discrediting and insulting Zonians made no difference. They believed their ends justified their means. We will never know whether ratification of the treaties might have failed, if not for these reporters' willful interference and slanted stories.

Twenty senators who voted for the treaties were up for reelection that November of 1978. Thirteen of those senators were not re-elected, but America had lost a piece of itself. As for me, I had lost my trust in our political system, but worse than that, my family and I had lost our home.

51

In 1989, after repeated malicious acts by Panama's General Manuel Noriega against the people of Panama and Americans still living in the Canal Zone, U.S. President George H. W. Bush acted decisively. On Friday, December 15, General Noriega declared a state of war between Panama and the U.S. The following day, Panamanian Defense Force (PDF) soldiers shot and killed a Marine Corps lieutenant, and some other PDF soldiers savagely beat a U.S. Navy lieutenant and his wife. On Tuesday, December 19, President Bush launched the invasion known as "Operation Just Cause" to oust Noriega and restore Panama's democracy.

For several months, I had been hearing from Dad that life in the Canal Zone was increasingly stressful. He had taken advantage of the early retirement package offered to many Americans who worked for the Panama Canal Company. Mom was still a civilian worker for the U.S. Army and had put in for several transfers, though none had come through. As soon as it did, they would move back to the States.

My parents weren't the only ones leaving the country. Dad wrote of riots, strikes, school closings, bank closings, and sporadic power blackouts. I imagined him suppressing a smile as he wrote that Mom had shot a hole in the dining-room table when she heard someone breaking in. It scared the person away though, and now Mom kept a cloth over the table.

The U.S. television networks covered the invasion and added commentaries and archival footage dealing with U.S.-Panamanian relations. The fall of the Berlin Wall just six weeks before was now forgotten. At one moment the world had been celebrating one country's reuniting and rejoicing in stories of families doing the same. At the next moment, in another part of the world, a country was splitting and divided loyalties were devastating families.

A few years earlier, Craig and I had moved our young family to Florida to live near Debi and her family and two years after that, Craig and I divorced. I enrolled in college to finish my degree to become a teacher. My sister Margie and her family lived in Germany, where her husband was stationed in the Army. Connie and her family lived in Nebraska, where her husband served in the Air Force. All of our dreams of returning to live in the Canal Zone vanished. Watching the loss of a way of life play out on TV was hard to comprehend and heartbreaking.

Within three days the fighting ended, but lives were forever changed. Ten years afterward, the Carter Treaty would be implemented and Americans would have no further claim to the land. Yet no matter what happened, I would always be a Canal Zone daughter.

EPILOGUE

In 2004, Dad, Mom, Connie, and I traveled back home to Panama. It was my first time back in over twenty years. Steven, my 16-year-old son, came with us. We rented a Buick and for twelve days, we were tourists.

Our family home in Bougainvillea was gone, the whole street replaced by a major highway. No longer did a military gate with confident MPs guard the entrance to Fort Amador, our former neighboring U.S. military base. Stately mansions replaced many houses where commanding officers once lived.

The Causeway now had cement sidewalks running down its length to an abundance of newly painted tourist shops and bright restaurants. Luxury yachts and sailboats filled a new marina where friends and I had spent long hot weekend nights talking, partying, and celebrating when it was still a graveled turnaround at the end of the road and beginning of the Canal.

Dad drove us through Balboa, where Panamanian businesses dotted areas once reserved for U.S. interests. New development marred the memories I cherished. Buildings that had housed Canal Zone operations were now vacant, yet stood as reminders of the colossal contribution of that small group of Americans who had served proudly for seventy-four years.

I left Mom, Dad, and Connie in Balboa to explore and drove the rental car with my son to Miraflores Locks. Together Steven and I watched ships go through the massive chambers, then visited the new museum that documents the history and advances of the Panama Canal. Nostalgic, I touched photographs of Americans and Panamanians working side by side—colleagues, friends, brothers. Steven studied the exhibits intently, fascinated by the ingenuity of man.

The next morning the five of us visited Summit Gardens and zoo exhibits maintained by the Smithsonian Institute. That afternoon we drove into Gamboa, right up to our old home to find it lifeless and empty. Connie tried the doors. They were locked, so we peered through the windows. The kitchen corner where Harry's cage used to be was empty, but time had not blacked out his familiar cackling laughter. The old wooden bench Dad had made years before was still secured to the wall—a lasting reminder that my family once lived there.

No one in the car spoke as Dad drove us slowly by the ghostly houses. A few of them were unexpectedly filled with life. Some were residences of workers in the dredging division of the new entity, Panama Canal Authority. A few more may have belonged to scientists, explorers, and adventure-seekers. But with a preponderance of empty houses, the Gamboa neighborhoods seemed bleak and lonely.

We parked beside the old Gamboa Movie Theater and walked up the outside cement stairs. Dad tried that door, to find it locked as well. Mom peered through the window screens and we did, too, wondering if the bats missed the beam from the projector that used to stir them to begin their nightly wanderings.

From there, we walked the few steps to the pool, neglected and empty of water and laughing children. The cement was crumbling at the pool's edge. "Remember how scary it was to jump off the tower?" I said, to no one in particular. Lost in her own memories, Connie nodded.

"You jumped from *there*?" Steven marveled. "I'll bet that was a lot of fun."

The following day, we drove to the Atlantic Side to visit Fort San Lorenzo, now registered as a World Heritage Site. The thick jungle was reclaiming the solitary road. No longer maintained by the Americans, sections of the road were almost impassable, with missing chunks of pavement. Carefully, Dad steered the car through the cracked asphalt. No cars came or went in this abandoned area, so there was no one to call if our car broke down. We were on our own.

From the back-seat window as we passed, I stared intently at the massive rambling vines and encroaching mangrove roots that separated the road and the Canal. Finally I saw the familiar rock formation jutting from the boulders, the one that was our landmark. The ocean still crashed against the rocks as if nothing had changed.

"Stop the car, Dad," I said. I rolled down the car window and pointed. "Look, Steven. See that rock shaped like a submarine?"

Sticky humidity sucked the air-conditioned coolness from the car. Heavy moisture weighed down our lungs. Tiny beads of sweat bubbled up on our faces.

"Yeah, I see it," he drawled. "Close the window. It's suffocating out there."

I rolled the car window up and smiled. Oddly I missed this torturous heat. We drove on through the eerie and uniquely peaceful jungle, Steven shrugged back in his seat—but I knew he was impressed. This was worlds away from anything he'd experienced before.

We reached the ruins of the old Spanish fort and stood atop the cliff where the Chagres River leads into the majestic Atlantic Ocean. Not missing a beat, just as he'd done when I was seven, Dad told Connie, me and now my son stories of pirates, gold and Spaniards. Mom smiled.

"Come here, Steven," Dad said as he walked over to the line of towering trees at the jungle's edge. He grabbed a vine hanging from a tree and used his pocket knife to cut into it. "If you know what you're doing," he told his grandson as he'd told me years ago, "you never have to go without fresh water in the jungle."

Clear water poured from the vine. "You can drink this, you know," Dad said, and took a sip. So did my son. I watched from a few feet away, wanting to freeze this moment in time.

Back in Gatun, we ate lunch at the Cristobal Yacht Club. I was relieved to find it still there, though there were only few patrons. Mom led us to a seat by the windows facing a picturesque view of sailboats tethered to their moorings and bobbing gently on the swells. Too soon, our meal was over.

"It's a long drive. Let's go back," Dad said. We climbed back in the car. Dad turned down a street along the Canal lined with a row of typical former Canal Zone houses. The emptiness of the familiar birdhouse dwellings seemed to reflect the loss of all that I once called home.

Dad stopped at one of the houses. His eyes misted as he remembered the first house where we'd lived. Once again, he told the story of how we had come to live in this little-known part of Central America. We were all silent when Dad turned the car around and the house disappeared from our view.

We drove on, paralleling the manmade wonder of the Panama Canal. At last, I broke the silence.

"I was going to raise my family here, too." I said.

Dad nodded. Mom, too. Connie's silence spoke volumes. She, like my other sisters, had also planned to raise her family here.

"I would have loved it here," Steven said.

"You really would have, son." I said. "It was an amazing

place to live. I was one of the lucky ones." One day I will bring my other grown children here and, I hope, my grandchildren. I want them to know and experience the Canal Zone history that was my history, too.

Connie and Mom leaned together and squished me in the back seat. Then together, we looked out the car windows to watch another ship pass through the great Panama Canal.

Sources

Bohning, Dan. "'Sickout' Almost Shuts Panama Canal." *Miami Herald*. March 17, 1976.

"Sickout Was Desparate Attempt to Be Heard." *Miami Herald*. March 22, 1976.

Broder, David. S. "The Press Is Guilty of Consumer Fraud." *Washington Post*. June 3, 1979. p. D-1.

Doeschner, John. "The People Caught in No-Man's Land." *Tropic Magazine* (*Miami Herald*). December 12, 1976.

Knapp, Herbert and Mary. *Red, White and Blue Paradise*. San Diego: Harcourt Brace Jovanovich, Publishers. 1984.

Lee, R. "Politics: Presidential Campaign Debate Between Gerald R. Ford and Jimmy Carter: Debate #2-Foreign Policy. October 6, 1976. http://www.historyguy.com/politics/presidential_debate_no2_1976.html.

Rasen, Edward. "The Panama Canal Sellout," *Penthouse*. November 1979.

Siegelman, Jim. "Playboy Interview: Geraldo Rivera." *Playboy*, November, 1978. www.canalzonedaughter.com.

Printed in the USA
CPSIA information can be obtained
at www.ICGtesting.com
LVHW042045270224
772984LV00044B/256